*Faux Real: Fear or Faith, You Cho*c incapacitating power of fear, u what fear is, and thus squelching its ɴoɪu. ᴀoᴜ... , words help us bring what is dark and hidden to light. His real-world application illustrates how to overcome fear with faith, empowering us to step into the fullness of our lives.

—**LISA BEVERE**, New York Times bestselling author, Co-founder Messenger International

I am so excited about this book *Faux Real*, as it articulates the amazing story behind VIVE Church and its incredible founders, Adam and Keira Smallcombe. The Bible says, "Without faith it is impossible to please God" (Hebrews 11:6), but the Bible also says that "faith without works is dead." What I love about Adam and Keira's story is that it is one of faith with bold actions, resulting in a church that is revolutionizing its region and beyond. I highly recommend you read *Faux Real* to super-charge and activate your faith to take you into the promises of God for your life. A must-read!

—**JURGEN MATTHESIUS**, C3 San Diego senior pastor, C3 Americas overseer

Every once in awhile a book comes along that speaks about a subject you think you don't need to read because you are well-versed on its topic. If you pick up *Faux Real* by Pastor Adam Smallcombe and think that, you'd be wrong. And you would miss an amazing treasure! Adam's Jesus-centered, scripture-focused, real-life, insightful study on Faith and Fear in the book of Joshua is not just another book on this topic. Using his personal experiences to illustrate Bible principles, *Faux Real* is a handbook for conquering the fears of today by following Jesus into the future. I am encouraged and challenged, and you will be also.

—**GINI SMITH**, Churchome

Adam Smallcombe is a man of God who is bold enough to lead with authority and courage, but is grounded in the simplicity of his love for people. He cares deeply about God's church and God's people. This is a book that will help propel both into an everyday lifestyle of choosing faith - real authentic trust in God - over all the obstacles that want us to choose fear.

—**MACK BROCK**, Worship artist & songwriter

If you read this book, I think it will fundamentally shift your paradigm on making big life decisions and navigating toward your purpose. Adam tackles the epidemic that paralyzes so many in our generation with indecision and that, if left untreated, will derail you from the purpose God is calling you to. That epidemic is fear. Adam has a way of dissecting the various facets of fear and provides very practical tools to overcome it. By the end of this book, I believe you'll have the tools and the confidence to choose faith over fear in whatever circumstance. The choice is yours!

—**VADIM LAVRUSIK**, Video product pioneer (leading product at YouTube; Facebook Live co-creator)

Being on one of the biggest platforms in America comes with high responsibility. Those responsibilities are a blessing. However, with all the responsibilities comes fear. Fear of failure, fear of not being good enough, and fear of leading future generations on a Godly path. This book has helped me embrace those fears and hand them over to God. It has helped me become a better leader and mentor. Just as Pastor Adam says... I don't have to face these fears alone, and neither do you! God is by your side!

—**BRADLEY PINION**, San Francisco 49ers

FAUX REAL

FEAR OR FAITH. YOU CHOOSE.

ADAM SMALLCOMBE

DEDICATION

Keira, Madiha, Tali and Zara...

You are the most adventurous beauties I know.

You epitomize what it means to be risk-takers.

You model audacious faith.

You are truly the most courageous and fiercely passionate women I know.

Your wild belief in me and your unwavering commitment to the purpose of God inspires me.

Thank you for being my squad.

TABLE OF CONTENTS

FOREWORD
BY DR. PHIL PRINGLE

I'm thanking God for this book. *Faux Real* is so needed by so many in a world of uncertainty, anxiety, fear and doubt, which all lead to false perceptions and uneasy imaginations. All of us feel the onslaught of fear, but right here, Adam has equipped us with the revelation that fear has no foundation, and if we can find that switch for our faith, then we will make it through the worst anxieties we will ever face. Once we start believing, our perceptions radically change from intimidating us to us overcoming the things we fear.

I've had the distinct pleasure of knowing Adam and Keira for many years. Books such as this come from a journey of faithfulness as much as of faith. One of the criteria I have in choosing leaders is the question "Do I want more of this kind of person?" As a church planter and someone who only wants the kingdom of God to increase and expand, my answer with this couple is a definite yes! The kingdom needs more leaders like them.

Adam is a great man of faith. He and Keira have proven this in stepping out from Australia to California to start a church from zero. They have raised up an incredible team of amazing ministers in his congregation. His faith has stepped out in starting new congregations already. He is well qualified to speak with authority and authenticity on the matter of believing. His candid and funny stories tell it like it is, that all of us must find our faith. I love the fact that Adam tells all and doesn't attempt to disguise the fact that he has faced serious days of panic and fear. Faith is never the absence of fear. It's believing in spite of the anxieties, the fears, and the doubts. Certainly, Adam has managed to navigate those waters. In fact, doubt and fear are part of the journey of faith. Without them faith would have no cause to rise!

I know that as you read this your own real faith will grow.

INTRODUCTION

In Bible college, I remember one particular lecturer asked the class a question that intrigued me: what character in the Bible did we identify with the most?

Looking back on my college days, I now realize why I couldn't answer the question at that time. It wasn't because I didn't know enough Bible characters. Raised in church, I knew the stories of Noah, Jonah and King David like the back of my hand. It was simply because I didn't really have enough life experience to fully connect with the fear and frustration these characters had to face.

If my lecturer were to ask me the same question now, I would confidently say Joshua. Joshua was certainly a man who had a heart after God and followed after great leadership. At the same time, he was one who had to overcome fear and opposition as he led God's people into new territory. Joshua is the Bible's poster child for facing off with fear and being forced to find faith for himself and an entire nation.

For me, the process of planting a church in a new country certainly has provided the platform for facing off with fear. Fear, like a force, holds us back and locks us out of what God calls us to do. At the same time, I have found that leading people will not only require us to find faith for ourselves but to show others the path that we had to forge. That pathway isn't always as simple as it sounds or as poetic as it's preached. Sometimes we can find ourselves stuck in certain seasons of life, struggling to progress under the weight of fear. But the Bible says to fight the good fight of faith. In my experience, that fight often involves overcoming fears that we would sooner run from.

This book was originally birthed out of a sermon series I preached to my church that has had a resounding effect on us as a community. The contents are a series of teachings that are continuing to take us deeper in our trust in God and are tested through the trials of church planting. While everybody faces off with different fears, I believe the tools God gives us through His Word are universal. As this is my first book, the process has required me to be more vulnerable than I expected, but I hope that my transparency and vulnerability will produce incredible victory in your life.

It is my prayer that we will find some tools to help us find faith in the midst of our own fear as we follow the journey of Joshua and the Israelites into the promise of God and draw from their real experiences.

1

FAUX FEAR

Now Jericho was tightly shut up because of the Israelites.
No one went out and no one came in.
Then the Lord said to Joshua, "See, I have delivered Jericho
into your hands, along with its king and its fighting men.
March around the city once with all the armed men.
Do this for six days.
Have seven priests carry trumpets of rams' horns in front of
the ark.
On the seventh day, march around the city seven times,
with the priests blowing the trumpets.
When you hear them sound a long blast on the trumpets,
have all the people give a loud shout;
then the wall of the city will collapse
and the people will go up, every man straight in."

JOSHUA 6:1-5 (NIV)

June 3, 2000, is a day etched in history for its monumental significance. I'm certain.

For most it was an ordinary day, a day like any other. Yet for me it was historic, a day like no other. It was a victorious day when fear was finally overcome, a day that marked the end of one era and the beginning of a new one—a day when the evidence of God's favor was realized.

It was the day that I finally started dating my wife, Keira!

Keira and I had been friends for some time. In fact, I had spent a few years stuck in what is known as the friend zone; so now that I had made it out, the transition from friendship to dating was a little awkward at first. You see, when you hang out as friends, things are simple; but as an official couple, there is a whole lot more pressure.

For instance, I remember our first date as a couple. I had made a reservation at a fairly expensive restaurant and even planned to pick her up in my dad's car to enhance the experience. I had asked her to be ready at 6 pm and to go ahead and dress nicely.

Now I had been to Keira's house many times before as friends, but this time I was more nervous than I had ever been. I can remember walking up the footpath and knocking on the front door. Anxiously I waited on the porch, excited to see my new girlfriend. I could hear the sound of her high heels on the wooden floor inside as she made her way to the door. This was going to be a great night.

The handle twisted, and the door opened up. There she was, smiling, standing before me. My eyes adjusted to the sudden change of lighting that also burst through the open door, and to my surprise, I realized she was wearing a hideous purple faux-fur animal skin coat!

I stood there staring, startled, unsure of what to do and—even worse—unsure of what to say. A thousand thoughts were flying through my head all at once. On one hand, I knew I had to open up with a compliment—please, I had some game. But on the other hand, my mind was screaming at me to not encourage this wardrobe choice. I panicked in the moment and blurted out the first thing that I could think to say: "So, are we going to a costume party?"

Her face dropped from a pleasant smile to pure shock. Without saying a single word, she slowly closed the door in front of me.

From Keira's perspective, she looked fabulous. I don't think she appreciated my perspective. Maybe you've heard the saying "perception is everything." Well, I learned firsthand that day that maybe it is not always everything!

What I did discover, however, is that your perception certainly does determine your reception. In other words, you could say that when it comes to the topic of fear in our life, perception plays a pivotal part.

Let me qualify this book from the start and say that instead of claiming to be an expert in the area of faith, I'm coming from the place of being experienced in the arena of fear. In the journey of starting VIVE Church, we've had the privilege of navigating all kinds of fear that often surface when stepping out for God: fear of failure, fear in the form of anxiety, and just plain fear of the unknown.

Don't get me wrong; in many ways we were full of faith. We had sold everything in Australia, bought one-way plane tickets to San Francisco, and stepped out into the unknown. Yet each step of the journey was like opening another door to fears that we could never have anticipated.

From the fear of having enough finances and attracting enough people to the very real fear in our own capability, I like to say that we started VIVE Church with little money, fewer people, and no clue what to expect. And let me tell you, this is the perfect recipe for fear.

But as I said before, I consider it a privilege because what I know to be true is that the purpose of God often attracts opposition. Opposition comes in many different forms but always stands in our path like a large fortified wall: a wall of fear that blocks you and holds you back from what God has promised you, or keeps you stuck in a certain season of life.

"THE PURPOSE OF GOD OFTEN ATTRACTS OPPOSITION.

These walls create doubt around your life; they can intimidate you and can even cause you to question everything. There are walls that you can see plainly and somewhat prepare for, but then there are the unexpected walls that take you by surprise.

I have found that all of these walls can actually serve as the very indicator and confirmation that you have made God's calling a higher priority than your own comfort.

When we excitedly responded to God's call to start a church, we did not realize that what lay ahead were a series of walls: walls of opposition that we would have to overcome and that God would ultimately use to shape us into the people He needed for the task. The walls we faced were walls of anxiety, walls of uncertainty, walls of frustration and fear. Yet what we see now on the other side of those walls is that God's plan for growing the church was just as much about Him growing us.

If I was asked to explain how the call of God works in our life, I would have to say that God's calling is realized through overcoming obstacles by way of finding faith in the midst of fear. Fear comes in different forms and affects people in different ways, but it is universal to everyone, and all of us have to battle it. Whether you're starting a church, a business, a new job, or even a new school year, the simple element of the unknown can produce enough fear to block you from even beginning. Fear is crippling and has the power to immobilize even the most seemingly confident person. Fear is responsible for most startups failing before they even begin. Fear works within the framework of our future but draws ammunition from our present and past. No one is immune to its attack.

> **"FEAR WORKS WITHIN THE FRAMEWORK OF OUR FUTURE BUT DRAWS AMMUNITION FROM OUR PRESENT AND PAST. NO ONE IS IMMUNE TO ITS ATTACK.**

Another way to say it would be that fear loves to intimidate us and prevent us from moving forward. It does this by using our past failures, regrets, mistakes, shame and even our present pain to cause us to second guess each step that we might make in the future.

Sitting on a plane, somewhere between our past and our future, was when the gravity of church planting first hit me. We were on our way to California from Sydney, and I can remember glancing at the screen embedded into the headrest in front of me that was tracking our flight. We were positioned over the Pacific Ocean at about the halfway point in the trip. I looked across the row and saw my wife and three daughters all asleep and leaning on each other.

Right at that moment fear gripped me and pinned me to my chair. A voice in my head said, "What have you just done?" I knew that voice all too well; it had tried to stop me before. But this time I could not ignore it as I had previously. I had just left everything I knew—security, comfort and assurance—and was headed to a huge unknown.

The plane was dark, so no one seemed to notice that I was having a major panic attack. I squeezed the armrest as if to hold on for my life. That voice spoke again: "You've done it now. You've wrecked your daughters' lives."

Thoughts bombarded my mind: *What had I just done? Maybe I did just make a huge mistake? Who am I to think that God would use me? What experience did I have? What qualifications? What was I doing?* I was deathly afraid.

I grabbed my backpack and reached for my Bible like it was the only lifeline I had. Before I even got to it, another much calmer voice spoke and said, "On the other side of your faith step will be countless lives that will be forever thankful."

Instantly the fear subsided. I was reminded that this whole thing was not my idea anyway, but it was God's. Faith filled my thoughts again. I realized in that moment that, for the journey ahead, I needed to figure out some way of keeping my focus on God or this was not going to work.

Fear is ferocious, and it is no respecter of persons. It finds strength in confusion, influences our decisions, and occupies more of our thought life than we would ever want to admit. But can I tell you that fear also has a rival that, when discovered, determines the difference between victory and defeat? My hope is that as we walk through this book together and identify the different walls of fear that hold us back, we will also find the faith that's available to us to overcome any obstacle that life might bring.

PERCEPTION

My daughters, and those who know me well, can tell you how much I like a good movie. One movie I recently watched with my girls was the movie called *After Earth* with Will Smith and his son Jaden. The movie is set in the future in a post-apocalyptic era where their spaceship has crash-landed on a now hostile planet Earth, and they are forced to survive. It's amazing. Now, the movie is high action and has you on the edge of your seat a number of times, but what made the movie for me was one scene in particular. It's the scene when Kitai (Jaden Smith) is stuck, paralyzed by fear at the task set before him. His father, Cypher Raige (Will Smith), knows that Kitai needs to move in order to survive, so he breaks down for him conceptually what fear is by saying,

The only place that fear can exist is in our thoughts of the future. It is a product of our imagination, causing us to fear things that do not exist at present and may not ever exist. That is near insanity. Do not misunderstand me, danger is very real but fear is a choice.

(WILL SMITH IN AFTER EARTH)

Will Smith in many ways articulates what I call faux fear: fear that is derived from things that do not actually exist. These are anxieties around what could be, or what would be, but are not yet. I'm talking about particular perceptions that we have concerning others, perceptions about ourselves, and the way we perceive the atmosphere around us. These fears are certainly real in the feelings and the emotions they produce but are faux in the fact that they are manufactured by the enemy to keep us stuck in life.

Fear happens to be the number-one tool that the enemy uses against believers, but it is not always as evident as you think. At the same time, fear doesn't always manifest itself as a heart-palpitating, throat-closing, body-sweating visceral response either. In fact, fear most often operates in the landscape of our thoughts and minds and aims to bring our identity into question. This is done through the platform called perception.

It's your perception of a certain circumstance or situation that holds the power to see it as positive or negative. It's the perception you have of yourself that can determine your confidence level and how you respond to others. There is so much power in perception that, if mismanaged or left unattended, it can be dangerous to the believer.

We see an example of this in scripture with the apostle Paul. In his letter to the Corinthian church, he challenges their perceptions with a defense argument of sorts concerning the complaints against him. There were those in the church who referred to Paul as a "paper apostle"—alluding to the fact that he seemed strong in letter but weak in person. Paul could have easily allowed their perceptions of him to determine his influence and effectiveness, but this is the resilient apostle Paul we are talking about: Paul, who was commissioned by God with the task of taking the gospel to the Gentiles; Paul, who would take a beating for his faith, get kicked out of a city, dust himself off, and then walk straight back in and start preaching again. This is Paul.

And so what we see is Paul, instead of conforming to their perception, confronting them by writing the following:

By the meekness and gentleness of Christ, I appeal to you—I, Paul, who am "timid" when face to face with you, but "bold" when away! I beg you that when I come I may not have to be as bold as I expect to be toward some people who think that we live by the standards of this world.

(2 CORINTHIANS 10:1-2, NIV)

There were troublemakers in the church referring to Paul as a mere spiritual guide or instructor instead of recognizing his apostolic authority. The apostle knew that how you perceive someone is how you receive them, and therefore makes it clear that while you have "ten thousand guardians in Christ, you do not have many fathers" (1 Corinthians 4:15, NIV).

This adjustment of perception was critical for Paul. His authority was being challenged and his character was being questioned, but if they were going to receive from him, then it mattered greatly how they perceived him. This is often the battleground of a leader and is an easy target for the enemy. If he can get you to second guess yourself through what others say or imply, then he has already won the battle. This is called spiritual warfare.

Paul knew all too well that spiritual warfare is predominantly a matter of perception around one's identity and is in fact what we have been fighting for since creation. Man originally lost dominion in the garden when Eve's identity was questioned. The Bible tells us that Satan came to the woman and told her, "For God knows that when you eat of it your eyes will be opened, and you will be like God, knowing good and evil" (Genesis 3:5, NIV).

Satan attacked the perception Eve had of herself and the perception she had of God. And so we see in this interaction that the devil tricked her because she was already in fact like God. Truth be told, she was made in the very image of God. In other words, the devil had confused her own perception.

Engaging in spiritual warfare is not just having an overly mature prayer language but obtaining a correct perception of the power and authority of Jesus.

Paul knew all too well that the enemy's plan against the church and against you and me is to block you out of God's blessing. The devil does not possess the power to keep you out of the kingdom of God, but if he cannot keep you out then he certainly wants to prevent you from progressing in your walk with Him. This is because the enemy knows that when a believer grows in their knowledge of God, they develop a correct perception of the personality of God and themselves. This, my friend, is when we become dangerous to the kingdom of darkness. This is what Paul considered spiritual warfare.

He goes on to write to the Corinthians:

For though we live in the world, we do not wage war as the world does. The weapons we fight with are not the weapons of the world. On the contrary, they have divine power to demolish strongholds.

(2 CORINTHIANS 10:3-4, NIV)

Paul uses the word "strongholds," which simply refers to the lies and deception of the enemy that have been allowed to build up in our minds, creating a fortified wall against ourselves. These are wrong thoughts and negativity that only perpetuate a deeper fear as they cloud our judgment concerning ourselves. As Paul indicates in this passage, the way to overcome these strongholds is to identify the truth amidst the chaos: identifying the weapons you have that are divine, or better still, allowing God to give you His perspective of you.

PERSPECTIVE

I can remember my first visit to Nashville. A couple of our team were there for a quick overnight conference. Other than being surprised at the amazing coffee we found, what impacted me about Nashville was one particular Uber driver. She was an African-American woman with a spectacular Southern accent who was loving life in the country music capital. As we were driving to our destination, she was voluntarily giving us the history, the hot spots, and all the highlights of her beloved city. It was both passionate and educational. I had never seen someone so vocally in love with their city before. Out of curiosity, I asked her what seemed to me like a logical question, a question that I considered simple but evoked a somewhat aggressive response. I said, "Ma'am, are you from Nashville or did you move here?"

She looked at me through the rearview mirror and said in a slow but stern voice, "Sir, what do you take me for? I am an originator, not a duplicator!"

She was preaching to me, and she didn't even mean to. Right at that moment I realized that too many of us are living like duplicates of something or someone else—not living confident, bold and courageous like we have been originally designed but like a product of fear and intimidation. We so often live intimidated and pushed around by perceptions that oppose us. You see, the devil is a duplicator and a counterfeit. Only God is the originator and designer of the real you. It's His voice that matters most. It's from His perspective that we need to see.

Let me repeat what I stated at the beginning of this book: perception is certainly important, but it's not everything. I say this because there is another element that influences the perceptions we have. It's called perspective.

Let me explain this for you as scholarly as I can.

Our perception in life is built from our perspective of life. In other words, perspective is defined as one's particular point of view, whereas perception is how one interprets that point of view. The order is important. A correct perspective is in fact critical to developing a healthy perception. That's why a partial perspective can develop a poor perception of yourself and others.

There is no greater example of this than what we see with the emergence of social media. I'm not about to go on a clichéd rampage against social media as you might be expecting. In fact, I minister in the social media capital of the world, so I actually have a deep affinity with social media. But as with anything that requires you to fill out a profile, with the wrong perspective it can end up profiling you!

Social media provides platforms to express your desired persona through the profiles you construct and build. This personal profile is built from the pictures you post and even the frequency in which you post them. These are all elements that play into the personal presentation of you.

Now, here's where it becomes problematic. Based purely on the level of activity, or even inactivity, you receive, you begin to analyze how people perceive you. This is dangerous when it drives you to a place where your questions become more than "Why don't people like my pictures" to "Why don't people like me?" What started out as harmless now has your identity in question.

An incorrect perspective will give the enemy the platform of comparison, intimidation and confusion, allowing him to create strongholds in our life—fears that are not real but are like a faux wall holding us back from progressing in the purpose of God. These faux walls are difficult to see and are the very reason why a correct perspective is essential to seeing what is not always visible.

Allow me to unpack this even more through a real-life example. Like most parents, we have had to navigate the classic case of kids being afraid of the dark. And as a parent, it can be extremely frustrating trying to explain to your child that there is absolutely nothing to be afraid of when they have opposing thoughts in their mind. I can remember one such night when one of our daughters was having a hard time going to sleep, and I was listening as my wife was helping our daughter with her perspective. She said something brilliant like she often does. She said, "Do you know what fear stands for? It stands for False Evidence Appearing Real."

Wow! I thought that was brilliant. I'm not sure if it

helped our daughter sleep at all but I quickly found a pen and wrote it down:

False Evidence Appearing Real

This is faux fear. Like a faux wall or a faux-fur coat, it appears real, but there is nothing substantial behind it. The apostle Paul used a specific word to describe the faux fears that come against us in verse 5 of 2 Corinthians 10. He says, "We demolish arguments and every pretension that sets itself up against the knowledge of God, and we take captive every thought to make it obedient to Christ" (2 Corinthians 10:5, NIV).

PRETENSION

The word "pretension" in many ways artfully describes what faux fear essentially is. It comes from the same Latin root as the words "pretend" and "imagination" and represents fear in the form of intimidation. Intimidation is often nothing more than a fictitious thought but is very real in the way that it keeps us captive. They are thoughts that set themselves up like walls in our mind opposing a true perception of God and of ourselves. Over time these walls become more and more fortified and end up keeping us captive to our own perpetuated fear. But as Paul describes in this passage, there is a weapon that can take captive what's been keeping you captive!

In the Old Testament we find one of my favorite Bible characters: Joshua. Joshua was a military leader under the oversight of Moses and displayed a passion and hunger for God's presence. Joshua was among the spies Moses sent into the Promised Land to give a report and was often found remaining around the tent of meeting long after Moses had met with God. In Joshua 6, we see one of the most well known Bible stories, which took place at a city called Jericho.

Most people would know that the story of Jericho involves God instructing Joshua to lead the army around the walled city seven times, and how that ultimately brought the Israelites a miraculous victory. But there are some hidden elements to this story that I believe can help us understand what kind of weapons Paul was talking about that allow us to take captive what keeps us captive.

In Joshua 6, we have a tense situation where the Israelites are now entering the Promised Land. The first thing they face upon entering the land is a blockage, a wall, a fortified city that the Bible describes as completely shut up. There was no way in and no way out. An intimidating enemy opposed them from entering into what God had promised them.

We then see that the Lord instructs Joshua with a series of sevens. They were to march around the city seven times, they were to be led by seven priests, and on the seventh day they were to blow seven trumpets.

Maybe you're like me and are wondering, *What is the significance of seven?* Well, seven in scripture is the number that represents totality, completion and perfection. Its emphasis in this story is God's way of reminding His people that He will bring about the victory on their behalf. Seven also represented the allotted period of time with which God wanted the Israelites to walk in silence, a specifically designed season of silence.

For Joshua, Jericho was not the only city he would overcome. But it was the most significant, because it was the first in a series of fortified cities. God was using Jericho to train Joshua how to win, not with natural weapons but with weapons that have divine power.

The wall that stood before them was certainly real. It was made from clay bricks, mortar and stone. But the wall that they had to overcome was the faux wall of fear and intimidation in their minds. This is where the victory is won and lost. The same fear that had talked them out of the Promised Land 40 years earlier was the same pretension that had set itself up against the truth of the promise now. This wall could not be demolished by natural weapons. This kind of wall could only be overcome by faith.

Maybe the fearful situation you are facing is real enough. Maybe it involves real people, real betrayal, or even real offense. But maybe what's keeping you captive is not the actual conversation, or even the people in the situation, but the thoughts you keep playing over in your mind and the dialogue you keep having with yourself.

What we see in the story of Joshua is that God instructs him with a peculiar strategy. It's one that most invading forces wouldn't dare to employ. The strategy was to not just walk around the wall seven times but also to walk in complete silence.

Can I just say that, in my experience, the way God works and the people He chooses to work through are often confusing to me. But knowing that His ways are higher than my ways helps me trust in His plan. The story of Joshua and Jericho really showcases the brilliance of God. God did not tell Joshua to employ standard military tactics. Instead, He commanded them to not say a single word.

Did you know that one of the weapons that the enemy fights with the most is your very own voice? He will have you speak negativity over your situations that will build up barriers and walls, blocking you from hearing what God wants to speak over you. And this is not a difficult task for the enemy. His ammunition is the limitations on our own lives that we see so evidently everyday.

Sometimes God needs to lead us in a season of silence for this reason. These seasons are when we do not fight the enemy on his terms and on his ground. They are seasons when we resist the desire to fight the enemy with the same weapons he is using on us.

Maybe this is as simple as spending a season not starting your day with social media but instead starting your day by looking in the mirror of God's Word. I wonder what voices you need to silence so that you can clearly hear what God is speaking over you. I wonder what you've talked yourself out of that God is wanting to walk you into.

The Israelites had 40 years of negativity, intimidation and fear of the occupants living in the Promised Land, and now they were facing a wall that held the potential to solidify that fear. For God to get them into a place where they could shout, He first had to teach them how to be silent. He was teaching them how to silence fear, knowing that, as a result, the season of silence would certainly strengthen their shout! As we silence negativity, as we silence comparison, and as we silence intimidation, it will only strengthen our shout of faith!

When it came to Jericho, it wasn't the shout that brought the walls down; it was faith. Hebrews tells us plainly, "By faith the wall of Jericho fell..." (Hebrews 11:30, NIV).

It was not by some kind of killer sound wave or resonance produced by a collective shout. No, victory came to Joshua and the Israelites by way of fixing their focus on what wasn't visible.

Another way to say it is, they didn't allow their perceptions to be built from what was visible but took their perspective from what was unseen.

Okay, so maybe that isn't any clearer.

Let me bring a bit more clarity to what I am trying to articulate. You see, what can be confusing to us is when what we see doesn't line up with what God said. I mean, it was certainly that way for Joshua upon seeing fortified Jericho. Check it out:

> Now Jericho was tightly shut up because of the Israelites. No one went out and no one came in. Then the Lord said to Joshua, "See, I have delivered Jericho into your hands, along with its king and its fighting men."
> **(JOSHUA 6:1-2, NIV)**

What Joshua saw before him was an ominous and intimidating wall: a wall of opposition that appeared impenetrable. Yet God says, "See, I have delivered Jericho into your hands." God was not interested in Joshua focusing on the opposition but instead developing a right perspective of the greatness of his God. I call it putting God's power in perspective.

It's easy for us to fixate on our flaws and focus on our fears; that requires zero faith. But to align our vision with what God sees requires a perspective of faith. This kind of vision comes from time spent in His presence where His voice becomes louder than any negativity.

As I mentioned earlier, Joshua was familiar with God's presence. The time spent seeking God long after Moses had left the tent of meeting was now producing a perspective of God's power that was bigger than his problem. It was God who would win the battle, and it was God who had the victory in hand.

Most often, fear and intimidation are overcome this way. Adjusting your perspective will change your perception. But what about others? How do you deal with other people's perceptions of you when you can't change or control their perspective? It could be your age, your background, or even the color of your skin. There are many different elements that can influence people's perception of us. This was certainly the case for me as a young minister.

I can remember in the first year of VIVE Church we had begun to see some incredible momentum. People were coming from all over and from all walks of life. We had young people, older people, pro athletes, entrepreneurs and company CEOs coming to service. To my delight, the church was growing rapidly.

One Sunday before service I was introduced to a professor from Stanford, a research scientist from NASA, and a local journalist all at once. I was introduced to the group, who were already in conversation, as the pastor of the church. I saw the immediate look of confusion on all their faces. I knew what they were thinking: surely this "kid" couldn't be the pastor? I was instantly intimidated and all too aware that my age and education were severely sub-par for this group of people.

As I was talking, or should I say rambling, I can remember thinking, *Adam, why are you being so weird?* I knew I was confirming their perceptions of me right there and then. As the service started, I had to retreat backstage. How was I going to preach in front of these people? What was I going to say? I was questioning my calling and questioning myself. I knew I had to pull myself together. I needed God's help—fast.

As I stood in the darkened hallway behind the stage curtain, I could hear the worship playing. What kept rolling through my head was 2 Corinthians 12:9:

> But he said to me, "My grace is sufficient for you, for my power is made perfect in weakness." Therefore I will boast all the more gladly about my weaknesses, so that Christ's power may rest on me.
>
> **(2 CORINTHIANS 12:9, NIV)**

God grabbed ahold of me and was adjusting my perspective. In fact, other scriptures began to come to mind:

> The Lord is on my side; I will not fear. What can man do to me?
>
> **(PSALM 118:9, ESV)**

So do not fear, for I am with you; do not be dismayed, for I am your God. I will strengthen you and help you; I will uphold you with my righteous right hand.

(ISAIAH 41:10, NIV)

What, then, shall we say in response to this? If God is for us, who can be against us?

(ROMANS 8:31, NIV)

Oh, and one of my favorites from youth ministry days:

Don't let anyone think less of you because you are young. Be an example to all believers in what you say, in the way you live, in your love, your faith, and your purity.

(1 TIMOTHY 4:12, NLT)

In this moment I discovered that the best way to overcome the perceptions others have about ourselves is to elevate God's perspective of us.

While perception isn't everything, perspective certainly is. Ephesians reminds us to set our sights on the reality of heaven. As you adjust your perspective, the perceptions you have about yourself and your circumstances change, and the pretensions you have concerning others dissolve. Faux fear is overcome by adjusting your focus with faith. When we take captive the thoughts that have captivated our focus, we begin to release the grip fear has held on our life by way of faith.

Over the pages of this book we will spend time exploring where this kind of faith is found and how we apply it, even while we are in the midst of fear.

Let's go!

day one

OPPOSITION

"The purpose of God often attracts opposition."

Walking in your God-given purpose involves leaving an area of comfort for a higher calling—but purpose doesn't always look like being a pastor. Some people are called to minister in their workplace while others are called to minister in their families. Either way, the journey of growing in your purpose will present opposition in the form of fear that can intimidate you and take you by surprise. The Bible reminds us in 2 Timothy 3:12 (NLT) that "everyone who wants to live a godly life in Christ Jesus will suffer persecution." In other words, the opposition that comes against us shouldn't surprise us. Instead, we should expect resistance since we have chosen to pursue God's assignment.

Think about the areas you feel called to minister during this season of life. What fears have you encountered when tackling this calling? What do the areas that fear manifests in tell you about the purpose of God on your life?

_____

_____

Fear often immobilizes us by "using our past failures, regrets, mistakes, shame and even our present pain to cause us to second guess each step that we might make in the future."

What elements from your past and present impact how you see the calling of God on your life and have stopped you from pursuing the next step?

_____

_____

_____

_____

_____

_____

_____

_____

_____

_____

_____

_____

_____

Thinking about all of the above - what might you have you talked yourself out of that God actually wants to walk you into?

---

day two

PERCEPTION & PERSPECTIVE

"Our perception in life is built from our perspective of life. In other words, perspective is defined as one's particular point of view, whereas perception is how one interprets that point of view. The order is important. A correct perspective is in fact critical to developing a healthy perception. That's why a partial perspective can develop a poor perception of yourself and others."

Think about a situation where you didn't have all the information and made a snap judgment. Maybe your children got into a fight and you accidentally yelled at the wrong one without knowing the context. Maybe you judged a coworker's email response speed before learning they were dealing with a loss in the family. Or maybe you simply ordered something off the menu without looking on the last page to realize they had specials for half the price! No matter what the situation, I am sure you understand the importance of having all the facts straight before responding.

In spiritual warfare, a "partial perspective" often looks like a misunderstanding of God, which leads to incorrect perceptions of both Him and yourself. By identifying the truth about God within the chaos of situations, we are able to break down strongholds of fear in our lives that hinder us from moving forward in our calling and responding to circumstances with the full perspective and right perception.

Think honestly about what your reactions to fear say about how you perceive God. What truths about God can you find within the Bible that challenge those perceptions?

_____

_____

_____

_____

_____

_____

_____

_____

_____

_____

When we don't have the right view of God, others' words are more weighted in our world than the words that He speaks over us, and it becomes all too easy to compare ourselves to those around us. The best way to overcome the perceptions others have about us—and the comparisons we make—is to elevate God's perspective of us.

What are some things that the Bible says about how God sees you?

_____

_____

_____

_____

_____

_____

_____

_____

_____

_____

_____

_____

_____

_____

_____

_____

_____

_____

_____

_____

_____

_____

_____

_____

_____

_____

_____

day three
PUTTING GOD'S POWER IN PERSPECTIVE

"One of the weapons that the enemy fights with the most is your very own voice."

Oftentimes, we are our own worst enemies. Nobody critiques our actions, motives, and results better than we do. That is why intentional seasons of silence can be so powerful. When God instructed the Israelite nation to walk around the walls of Jericho in complete silence, He was teaching them to silence any voice of negativity or unbelief that could have hindered their progress. In its place, they strengthened the shout of faith that would bring the walls tumbling down.

What voices do you need to silence so that you can clearly hear what God is speaking over you?

_____

_____

_____

Seasons of silence can be critical in establishing a vision that is based on God's promises. Aligning our vision with what God sees requires a perspective of faith that comes from time spent in His presence where His voice becomes louder than any negativity. There is no substitute for God's presence: it <u>reveals</u> His glory, <u>reminds</u> us of who He is and who we're called to be, and <u>removes</u> any pretensions in our lives that block us from receiving revelation.

How can you make time to be in God's presence more this week?

_____

_____

_____

_____

_____

_____

_____

_____

_____

_____

_____

The revealing, reminding, and removing that happen in God's presence cannot have effect unless we relent.

What are some ways you can be intentional about seeking God's presence and allowing Him to illuminate what He wants to do in that moment?

_____

_____

_____

_____

_____

_____

_____

_____

_____

_____

_____

_____

2

REAL FEAR

Then Joshua secretly sent out two spies from the Israelite camp at Acacia Grove.
He instructed them, "Scout out the land on the other side of the Jordan River, especially around Jericho."
So the two men set out and came to the house of a prostitute named Rahab and stayed there that night.

JOSHUA 2:1 (NLT)

Recently we had a birthday in our house. It was for my eldest daughter, but this was by no means a celebration for me.

That's because it was her fifteenth birthday!

For every father, the day that your daughter starts high school is the day you experience real fear. I mean, that is when parenting gets real. To make matters worse, Madiha is stunningly gorgeous, which certainly does not help a dad's state of mind, knowing that it will not be long before boys start knocking. What I'm also finding to be increasingly difficult is holding my daughters to the promise that I made them make when they were five years old to live with me until they are thirty!

Nevertheless, my ten-year-old twin girls, Zali and Zara, are hilarious when it comes to dealing with boys. One time they told me that a boy in school professed his love for Zali (this was on a Monday). That Thursday I picked them up from school and, as they got into the car, she told me "Dad, you're not going to believe it. Another boy likes me now. He also told me today."

I looked at her with a somewhat calm but confused face, as I tried my best to hide the fact that I was slowly starting to freak out. I said to her twin sister, "Another boy? Is this true, Zara?"

And Zara replied, "Yep, it's true! Them poor hearts be dropping like flies!"

This, my friends, is real fatherhood fear.

Now I'm being lighthearted while carrying the sober understanding that many of the fearful situations we face in life are, in reality, no joke. Maybe this is the case for you. Maybe you've experienced the kind of fear that is, frankly, no laughing matter.

I have found that when it comes to the area of fear in our life, beyond the walls of perception and imagination, there is another kind of fear that is difficult to ignore. It is what we could consider as undeniable and legitimate fear that acts as a gigantic wall in your life, stopping you in your tracks. I'm not just talking about a basic phobia like the fear of spiders; that's cute. I'm talking about the kind of fear that grips you and immobilizes you in life. I'm talking about the fear of rejection, the fear of a broken heart, the fear of losing everything you have built because of one bad decision, and even the fear of your past catching up with you.

This is what I consider real fear that comes from real circumstances and has real effect. Real fear are things like health fears from a negative diagnosis or maybe financial fears after being let go from your job. Maybe it's the fear of discrimination that is an ever-present reality within our generation. I'm talking about the kind of fear that presents real intimidation from actual opposition. And while we discussed fear in the form of false evidence simply appearing as real, I have to tell you that not every fear is fictitious.

In fact, regardless of whether you're facing faux fear or real fear, all fear draws its power from the same place. I have come to learn that fear finds its strength in what we do not know.

Maybe we could take a moment to peer behind the wall and see exactly where fear finds its strength, and at the same time, possibly discover some clues as to where we could find a deeper faith.

My seventh-grade teacher had a favorite quote, which was "knowledge is power." He would say it often in the hope that we would possibly be inspired to apply ourselves and learn the material he was teaching us. Some days it felt like he would say it on repeat like a broken record. One day he quoted it to the class, as he did most days, and was met with a response he was not expecting. A fellow student had obviously learned something from his dad and was just waiting for the right moment.

As soon as our teacher said his quote, the kid responded with, "Actually, sir, it's applied knowledge that is real power." This was one brave kid. We all held our breath, expecting our teacher to reprimand the witty remark, but to our surprise he could not refute it. Instead, from that day forward, our teacher had a slightly adjusted favorite quote.

Revelation is certainly powerful, but without its counterpart called application, its effect is limited. Fear often exists in the realm of the unknown. It draws its strength from our lack of knowledge and holds us captive to what we cannot control. There are several words we could use to describe this kind of fear: worry, dread, stress, doubt, angst, apprehension and especially anxiety. But no matter what name you give it, the effects on us are indisputably real.

I have met people who are so gifted that it is ridiculous. They have way more talent than I ever will but are so evidently limited by fear of man. They can sing better than most yet are too afraid to take the stage because of what people might think. As a leader I have had this conversation about fear often. I've tried convincing young people to not be afraid of what their friends might think. I have preached multiple series on it, done group Bible studies, and have even had one-on-one discussions around the topic. But after a while, I realized that no matter the amount of teaching I could give on a subject, what I could not do for them was actually apply it to their life. That part was completely up to them.

Let me say it this way: revelation will always require application if there is ever going to be real transformation.

Let's go a little deeper.

SURFACE SWAG

The question that I feel is most prevalent in today's society when it comes to spirituality would have to be around its application to real-world situations. I mean, does the Bible give us guidance when it comes to everyday life as we know it, or is it merely conceptual, only referencing the spiritual world? Better yet, how do we overcome fear—especially when situations get real?

The apostle Paul certainly had what we would call "real-world experience." In his letter to the church in Corinth, we find him in the middle of real opposition. He says,

> I do not want to seem to be trying to frighten you with my letters. For some say, "His letters are weighty and forceful, but in person he is unimpressive and his speaking amounts to nothing." Such people should realize that what we are in our letters when we are absent, we will be in our actions when we are present.
>
> **(2 CORINTHIANS 10:9-11, NIV)**

I have to applaud Paul's approach to the accusations against him here. He boldly confronted those who were challenging and questioning his apostolic authority and told them plainly that some of them had misunderstood his strength because of his style. They were being influenced by false teachers whom they were believing at face value. But Paul, even beyond defending himself, desired to take the church deeper than a surface swag. In other words, Paul was not about to let the Corinthians be influenced by superficial teaching. His concern came from the understanding that those who are overly impressed by mere appearances will be easily intimidated the same way.

> **THOSE WHO ARE OVERLY IMPRESSED BY MERE APPEARANCES WILL BE EASILY INTIMIDATED THE SAME WAY.**

Maybe you know somebody like this: those who are only surface deep? These people are always driven by desire and change their preference with every new product. They are the kind of people who are all about the latest workout one week, and then some new diet the next. They are always the quickest to jump onto the latest fad, and they will more than gladly tell you all about it too.

This may be an absurd assumption, but they appear to be the same people who quickly react to any doomsday news. I'm sure you know someone like this. Their Facebook feed is a constant stream of issues and agendas projecting the demise of society as we know it.

It makes me wonder: can being a fanatic for attention also cause you to be an addict to worry? This was the issue that Paul was trying to confront. Being the true father that he was, he came to the Corinthians with the goal of establishing a faith that was not simply surface deep. He wanted them to have a faith that was not dependent on favorable circumstances, but a faith that is found even in the most fearful of situations. This brand of faith can combat the kind of fears that aren't just a figment of your imagination. This kind of faith can overcome any obstacle life may bring.

But not all opposition needs to be avoided. There are some experiences that may not be favorable but will certainly be valuable in deepening your faith. I have realized that without certain life experiences, we run the risk of being sheltered or shallow and will not develop the endurance required to sustain us through life. As with lifting weights at the gym, resistance is necessary in developing strength.

Out of all the people I have spoken to in my life, there are possibly only a few conversations that I can distinctly remember. One in particular was my first real pastoral assignment. At the time, I was the youth pastor at our church, and I was enjoying the challenge of growing a ministry. I remember there was a college student who had been attending for several weeks who appeared to be somewhat awkward socially. He was respectful, honoring, and always offered to help with anything that needed to be done. But I had received a few reports from some of girls that he was being a little too friendly. In other words, when he would hug them he would hold on a bit too long.

I considered it my personal duty as the entrusted shepherd of the flock to bring correction to this behavior, but I was nervous. I had never done this before, and I honestly did not know what I was going to do. So I asked to meet with him over breakfast. On the way there, I rehearsed exactly what I was going to say. I didn't even wait to order when we sat down. Instead I began to preach at him about character and integrity and how we are meant to treat women. I was strong in my conviction, and boy did I let him have it. I used all kinds of examples and even referenced scripture in my speech. All the while, he sat there with a deeply remorseful look on his face. At the end of my rant I asked him what he had to say for himself.

He slowly looked at me and then apologized for any inappropriate behavior. I thought to myself, *Job well done, Adam.*

He then proceeded to explain his actions. He told me how he had not grown up in a normal home. In fact, he grew up on a drug farm. As a kid, his parents grew marijuana and ran an illegal business dealing drugs. He can remember always being afraid that they would get caught and that the police would take his parents away. Because of the secrecy of his parents' trade, they grew up in a remote location with no electricity or running water. He grew up hardly ever showering due to the lack of hot water, resulting in him being known as the stinky kid at school. Things went from bad to worse one day when his dad decided to leave them, and his mom decided she could not handle the responsibility, so she also left.

He continued to tell me story after story of growing

up alone and the rejection that he had felt. I sat there shocked, hearing some of the things he shared. He then explained to me that it was not until he stepped into church that he felt love for the first time: not just from God but also from the people in the church. The first Sunday he walked in he was greeted with a hug. Before the day he stepped into church, he could not remember ever having been hugged. It was his new favorite thing. He looked me in the eyes and said, "I guess I'm not very good at it."

I wanted to shrink into a hole. I felt like the most foolish and ignorant person to ever live. I read the entire situation from a surface level. I had attacked the situation from a partial perspective. I learned that day how dangerous assumption can be and how easily it can result in an overreaction.

This was not my favorite moment, but it has certainly been valuable in teaching me empathy and finesse. Countless situations like this have given me the experience I need today for the assignment God has me on now as a senior pastor. Nothing can grow without resistance—not a muscle, not a marriage, not a ministry. Truth be told, what we often consider as opposition, God sees as an opportunity to develop us in a deeper way.

SHUT DOWN

What we have learned from Joshua so far is that the people of God brought down the walls of Jericho with a shout of faith. But what might be helpful to know is where they found that faith. In Joshua 2, we have the setting to find the answer.

You see, Joshua is poised on the edge of the Promised Land, ready to take possession of what God was giving them. He is standing at the same place Moses had stood 40 years earlier when he commissioned the 12 spies to go into the land and bring back a report. Joshua had been one of these spies himself.

For those who know their Bible history, you would know that only two spies returned with a good report. The other ten reported the opposition they saw, which instilled fear in all the people. The mistake that Moses had made four decades earlier was listening to too many opinions and not an accurate report. And so, in a great display of strategy, we see that Joshua learns from the last time he was in this place and sends only two spies instead of twelve.

Joshua commissioned them, and he told them specifically to spy out the land—especially Jericho. He did this for a good reason too. Strategically, Jericho guarded the passageway between the Jordan Valley and the central hill country where you find Jerusalem and Bethel, and it also represented the opposition that had intimidated them last time.

The spies secretly made their way into the city and set up surveillance from the house of Rahab. But not too long after arriving their cover was blown. It says,

> But someone told the king of Jericho, "Some Israelites have come here tonight to spy out the land." So the king of Jericho sent orders to Rahab: "Bring out the men who have come into your house, for they have come here to spy out the whole land." Rahab had hidden the two men, but she replied, "Yes, the men were here earlier, but I didn't know

where they were from. They left the town at dusk, as the gates were about to close. I don't know where they went. If you hurry, you can probably catch up with them." (Actually, she had taken them up to the roof and hidden them beneath bundles of flax she had laid out.) So the king's men went looking for the spies along the road leading to the shallow crossings of the Jordan River. And as soon as the king's men had left, the gate of Jericho was shut.

(JOSHUA 2:2-7, NLT)

The city was shut and their access was restricted.

Now let's pause there for a moment because I need to show you something about spiritual warfare before we can move on with Joshua. Let me start out by saying that the devil does not necessarily attack you with a parking fine, as you might think. That's right, the devil probably did not cause your flat tire, and he probably is not ambushing you through the hectic traffic conditions you face on your daily commute. So often I hear people attribute their mildly inconvenient circumstance as the devil's attack on their life.

The devil's focus is way more sinister than your inconvenience. His objective is to steal your peace completely and to rob you of all joy; this is how he works. As we discovered in the previous chapter, what the enemy is most interested in is attacking your identity. My pastor, Phil Pringle, says it this way in his book *The Born Identity*:

Many of us are living with a spiritual kind of amnesia, forgetful of who we are. Negative

circumstances constantly send us the
message that we are less than what the New
Testament declares us to be.

(THE BORN IDENTITY, BY DR. PHIL PRINGLE)

This is because the devil knows that the most effective way to limit your influence is to come against your identity and distract you from the truth of who you are. When you don't know who you are, you also don't remember what you have access to. The Bible, however, reveals that, as children of God, we have all access—even into the very throne room of heaven.

Let me pull the curtains back on the plan of the enemy for a moment. You see, the devil doesn't want you to realize the access you have, because it's what he used to have. He had access to the throne room of God. He was in charge of worship. But he lost access when, instead of glory flowing through him, he desired glory flowing to him. As a result, the Bible tells us that he was thrown out of heaven. Jesus said, "I saw Satan fall from heaven like lightning!" (Luke 10:18, NLT).

Since that moment, he has been jealous of your access. So he has been doing all he can to distract you from what has been rightfully given to you.

Even before we started the church, one of the major areas of fear we faced was around finances. We knew that starting a church in a country where we could not work and earn an income because of visa restrictions was going to take a lot of money. Unfortunately, we did not have much compared to what was needed for the task. The little we had was mostly spent in simply moving to the United States. So you could say that the fear was real.

But what we quickly discovered as we held onto what God had spoken to us was that no matter the limitation we had connected to our earthly channels for resource, we had access to the resource room of heaven. We began to see God provide in ways that money cannot buy. I'm talking about deals with venues for church and housing for our family that would make anybody jealous.

I remember one time before we had officially launched the church I was talking to a friend from Australia who had stopped in San Francisco on his way through for work. We caught up for coffee and were chatting when he asked me what we needed most to launch the church. At that time we had been renting some pretty grungy sound equipment from a local music store, so the answer wasn't very difficult. I told him that what we really needed was about $80,000 worth of sound gear. He said, "Don't worry. God's got it."

While I did not fully understand what he was telling me in that moment, I completely agreed with him that God had the provision for the vision. A few weeks later, to our surprise, boxes and boxes of sound gear started arriving at my house, and we had our sound set up for the launch! It was another great reminder to us that we had access to a greater resource than our bank account indicated.

In the case of Joshua and the Israelites, the gate of Jericho was shut, eliminating access. Jericho was known as the great walled city and it was considered to be impenetrable. It had an inner wall as well as an outer wall. The walls were said to be so thick that they could hold chariot races on top of them. And of course the Israelites were afraid of the inhabitants who resided within these terrifying walls. Furthermore, it blocked their access to the promise God gave them.

However, this wall also provided God with the perfect setting to show Joshua that no matter what earthly limitation you might face, nothing can stop you from accessing the power of heaven. The passage goes on to say,

> Before the spies went to sleep that night, Rahab went up on the roof to talk with them. "I know the Lord has given you this land," she told them. "We are all afraid of you. Everyone in the land is living in terror. For we have heard how the Lord made a dry path for you through the Red Sea when you left Egypt. And we know what you did to Sihon and Og, the two Amorite kings east of the Jordan River, whose people you completely destroyed. No wonder our hearts have melted in fear! No one has the courage to fight after hearing such things. For the Lord your God is the supreme God of the heavens above and the earth below.
>
> **(JOSHUA 2:8-11, NLT)**

SAME SPACE

Right here we see a powerful passage on where faith is found. If you study scripture for some time, you will begin to notice certain themes and streams that repeat consistently throughout God's Word. One such theme is the constant elevation of sound over sight.

We see this with Elijah in the Old Testament. The entire nation had been in drought for three years when God spoke to the man of God and told him that He was sending rain. Elijah began to pray, but before he could see even one cloud in the sky, the Bible says that he heard the sound of a mighty rainstorm. Sound over sight.

We see this again with the disciples as they waited in the upper room. When Jesus ascended to heaven after the resurrection, He commanded them to wait for the Holy Spirit. As they waited in the upper room, Acts 2 tells us that they were met with the sound of a mighty rushing wind. After that, what appeared were what looked like tongues of fire. Sound over sight.

Even in creation we see this manifest. Genesis reveals that the world began with a sound from heaven: as God spoke, the world was formed. In fact, the story of Lazarus confirms this also. In John 11, what was visible was death. But Jesus spoke and, at the sound of His voice, what was dead came back to life. Sound over sight.

The Bible tells us that faith comes by hearing the uncompromising word of God. This is God's Word spoken, audible, heard. When fearful situations present themselves like an intimidating wall consuming your perspective, that is the time to speak God's Word over your circumstance. It's a spiritual tool that has practical and powerful results. Hebrews makes this spiritual and practical connection too. It says, "By faith we understand that the worlds were framed by the word of God, so that the things which are seen were not made of things which are visible" (Hebrews 11:3, NKJV).

In the story of Joshua, God's people were afraid of the enemy behind their walls. Yet, Rahab's testimony revealed something that encouraged them greatly. She reported on what the enemy had heard. They had heard about Joshua's God in action. They had heard how his God had parted the Red Sea and how an entire nation was delivered. They had heard about what happens to the enemies of Joshua's God. The enemy was terrified that Joshua and the Israelites might just realize how powerful their God really is.

The enemy is still terrified of that exact same thing today. He is afraid of God's people realizing how powerful our God actually is and what we are capable of as a result.

Jericho was a space, a city spanning about 10 acres. But it was not the size of the city that held intimidation. It was the unknown space beyond the wall that had them afraid. Was it militarized as much as it was fortified? Were its warriors as fierce and intimidating as the wall that surrounded it?

It's in this unknown space where fear most often resides for us too. Not knowing how long my finances are going to last. Not knowing if my marriage will break down like my parents did. Not knowing whether diabetes or cancer will get me like it has my relatives. Not knowing the stability of my job or the trajectory of my current career. Not knowing if I will be able to have kids one day, and if I do, will they handle bullying or will they face discrimination?

It's the unknown element of life that can cause us to hesitate and second-guess what God has spoken.

For Joshua, fear had resided in that unknown space of Jericho. But there is something else that is found in the unknown space. The passage goes on to say, "Then the two spies came down from the hill country, crossed the Jordan River, and reported to Joshua all that had happened to them. 'The Lord has given us the whole land,' they said, 'for all the people in the land are terrified of us'" (Joshua 2:23-24, NLT).

This unknown space that had held them back in fear for 40 years was now the same space that would spark their faith. Upon hearing the confession of the enemy, that they were afraid of God's people, Joshua found the courage to advance in the same space that had held him at bay.

Fear is found in the unknown space, but so too is faith. The same space that held fear for the Israelites was now the very same space that gave them the confidence to fight because of what they had heard. After peering behind the wall, and bringing down the enemies façade, they were reminded of the greatness of their God. Yahweh had brought them victories before, and He would do it again. He would fight on their behalf; they simply had to elevate the sound of faith over the fear that occupied their sight.

"FEAR IS FOUND IN THE UNKNOWN SPACE BUT SO IS FAITH.

Let me show you what faith sounds like:

For the Lord your God is the one who goes with
you to fight for you against your enemies to give
you victory.
(DEUTERONOMY 20:4, NIV)

Be strong in the Lord and in his mighty power.
(EPHESIANS 6:10, NIV)

From the Lord comes deliverance. May your
blessing be on your people.
(PSALM 3:8, NIV)

The horse is made ready for the day of battle, but
the victory belongs to the Lord.
(PROVERBS 21:31, ESV)

But thanks be to God! He gives us the victory
through our Lord Jesus Christ.
(1 CORINTHIANS 15:57, NIV)

Joshua learned the vital leadership lesson that
day of where faith is found, which gave him the
confidence to lead the nation to victory. Faith helped
them realize that what they had been afraid of was
actually afraid of them.

Let me remind you that faith does not eliminate
fear; instead, it gives you the courage to fight it.
God will often use fearful situations in our life to build
fortitude within us. He can use what we are afraid
of most as an opportunity to develop a greater trust

in Him. In many ways, God used the same fear that was locking Joshua out of Jericho to keep Joshua's enemy locked in.

Without fear there would be no fight for your faith. If you were to talk to great men and women of faith, I doubt they would tell you stories of success. Alternatively, they would share their struggles and tell you stories of what they had to overcome. This is what produces great faith.

The Bible refers to it as the testing of our faith. In the Bible, James tells us that growing in faith comes as a result of trials that we face in life.

Only as we apply the knowledge gained through these trials will we see a deeper strength developed in our lives. This is where spiritual principles meet practical application. This is where spirituality plays a pivotal part in our lives.

It makes me wonder, in what other ways could God use the fear that I face to bring me closer to Him? Does fear have a function beyond building our faith? Could it be that we need fear?

Let's find out.

day four
FAITH IN ACTION

*"Revelation will always require application if there is
ever going to be real transformation."*

Have you ever listened to a lecture or a sermon on
something you find particularly difficult and still have
never seen growth in that area in your life? That is
because unless we take actionable steps with the
knowledge we have been given, the effect of what
we have learned is minimal. Application matters. The
same is true with faith.

Real fear is powerful, because it deals in unknowns.
But real fear is what allows us to access a real faith
that we put to work in our lives. In Philippians 4:9
(NLT), Paul says to "[k]eep putting into practice all
you learned and received from me—everything you
heard from me and saw me doing. Then the God of
peace will be with you."

In other words, faith requires us to be obedient
to God's Word and faithful with what He has given
us. When we put faith into action, we can see true
transformation.

In the story of Joshua, it was the resistance of
those the Israelites came up against that made their
victories—by way of obedience to God's Word—so
significant. In the same way, the resistance you feel
in the form of real fears in your life (such as health

issues, financial struggles, or relational crises) is what develops the strength of our faith and gives glory to God when we ultimately overcome by being obedient to what He's told us.

Identify some real fears in your life today. How can you put faith to work in those circumstances through obedience?

_____

_____

_____

_____

_____

_____

_____

_____

_____

_____

_____

_____

As coming up against real fears causes us to build our faith, it brings us closer to God by highlighting new aspects of His goodness.

In the fear that you are currently facing, what facets could God possibly use to bring you closer to Him?

_____

_____

_____

_____

_____

_____

_____

_____

_____

_____

_____

_____

day five

ACCESSING YOUR INHERITANCE

"The Bible reveals that, as children of God, we have all access—even into the very throne room of heaven."

In this life there are real problems that cause real fear—sickness, disasters, loss of a job, or loss of a loved one. When we encounter tough situations like these, it can be hard to see a way out. Yet, that is likely because we forget what we have been given as children of God.

The Bible makes it clear when we come into relationship with Jesus that "together with Christ we are heirs of God's glory" (Romans 8:17, NLT) and that we have been given the "keys of the kingdom of heaven" (Matthew 16:19, NLT). This means that God has given us access to all power and authority in heaven.

Jesus himself said, "I tell you the truth, anyone who believes in me will do the same works I have done, and even greater works, because I am going to be with the Father. You can ask for anything in my name, and I will do it, so that the Son can bring glory to the Father" (John 14:12-13, NLT).

How does the revelation that you have access to

all power in the heavenly realms change how you view the real fears in your life?

_____

_____

_____

_____

_____

_____

_____

_____

_____

_____

_____

_____

_____

_____

Frequently, we struggle to combat the fears in our life because we forget what we have been given access to by God.

Instead of focusing on the fear that is blocking you, what can you remind yourself that you have access to by faith?

_____

_____

_____

_____

_____

_____

_____

_____

_____

_____

_____

day six

SOUND OVER SIGHT

"When fearful situations present themselves like an intimidating wall consuming your perspective, that is the time to speak God's Word over your circumstance."

The first function for speech was creation. In fact, it was the Word of God that created everything in the universe. Throughout the Bible, we continue to see the elevation of sound over sight.

Read the following chapters of the Bible and highlight the instances where sound is elevated over sight:

- Genesis 1: Creation
- 1 Kings 17-18: Elijah and the drought
- John 11: Lazarus's resurrection
- Acts 2: Pentecost

The Bible tells us that the power of life and death is in the tongue (Proverbs 18:21, NIV). In order to combat real fear, you should elevate the sound of faith over the fear that occupies your sight.

What scriptures can you speak over your life to increase the volume of faith today?

_____

_____

_____

_____

_____

_____

_____

_____

_____

_____

_____

_____

3

THE FEAR WE NEED

Joshua sent some of his men from Jericho to spy out the town of Ai,
east of Bethel, near Beth-aven.
When they returned, they told Joshua,
"There's no need for all of us to go up there;
it won't take more than two or three thousand men to attack Ai.
Since there are so few of them, don't make all our people struggle to go up there."
So approximately 3,000 warriors were sent,
but they were soundly defeated.
The men of Ai chased the Israelites from the town gate as far as the quarries, and they killed about thirty-six who were retreating down the slope. The Israelites were paralyzed with fear at this turn of events, and their courage melted away.

JOSHUA 7:2-5 (NLT)

"You're only as good as the people you hire."

This Ray Kroc quote, along with a sign that read "Clean as you GO," hung as one of many inspirational posters in the crew room of my first ever workplace. I was 15 years old and a proud employee of the highly reputable and globally recognized restaurant known as McDonalds.

Now I know that to some, the pay rate of $4.84 per hour is laughable, but as far as I was concerned I was making some serious cash. I grew up in a household that did not believe in allowance or pocket money. Every time we would ask my dad for allowance, he would simply remind us how he already allowed us to eat his food and sleep in his house. To be finally making my own money was pure freedom. And that's not even the best part. The best part about working at McDonalds back in those days was that as an employee you could eat all you wanted for free during your shift—I was in McNugget heaven.

Could life seriously get any better?

That was until I found out that one of my good friends from school also had a part-time job. He worked for a local surf shop and was being trained in the art of surfboard shaping. I mean, talk about putting things into perspective. He would tell us all about his cool and creative job, explaining that he was pretty much a modern-day artist expressing himself through the medium of foam and resin. Compared to flipping burgers, there seemed to be no contest as to who had the better job.

From that day forward I suddenly began to see my job for all its limitations and restrictions. Sure, I still got free McNuggets, but it was in no way as cool as shaping surfboards.

Later in the school year, when it came to work-experience placement, I decided that I was signing up for surfboard shaping. It was all that I thought about. I could not wait to start. For two weeks I was going to experience a new level of creativity and design. It was going to be amazing. To my surprise, however, my experience did not match my expectations.

You see, upon starting the work experience I realized quickly that my friend had somewhat embellished the perks of the job. He had painted the picture of artistry and discovery when it was actually the complete opposite. There was actually little to no freedom at all. Every surfboard was shaped to a predetermined template that was then mass produced. The entire workshop was filled with the toxic scent of resin and wax that would leave you with a migraine after just one hour. The workers were intimidating, the hours were strict, and it took me less than 3 hours to realize that I had made a severe comparison mistake. On my first day there I was already wishing I was back working the burger bar at the Big M!

That day I learned a very important life and leadership lesson: comparison kills contentment. If I was ever going to feel fulfilled or content in life, then I needed more than a career. I needed to figure out my *calling*.

REASON

As a pastor, the notion of calling is something I get asked about often. It's not really ever asked plainly, such as, "What is my calling?" It's often asked through a series of other questions. Let me just save some time and give you the top-five questions people ask when it comes to calling:

What am I meant to do with my life?

Who am I meant to marry?

What career path am I meant to take?

What school should we send our kids to?

Should we even have kids at all?

I think we ask these questions because success in life seems to be connected to having fulfilled our calling, right? So the question of calling can be contentious.

When it comes to our calling, I want to make sure you are aware that we certainly have an enemy that opposes us. The Bible makes that clear. But I wonder if most of the time the greatest threat we face could possibly come from ourselves.

As we saw from my earlier story, one of the biggest pitfalls to contemplating our calling is comparison. Comparison feeds your fear and starves your faith. This is somewhat a result of human nature. As humans we tend to be competitive, naturally wired to compete and compare. We do it even when we don't realize it, or we excuse it as something that it's not. A lot of supposed "inspiration" is just mislabeled comparison. It comes from feeding off another's calling and seeing what they do as more significant or attractive than what God has purposed you to do, which only ever diminishes our own calling.

"COMPARISON FEEDS YOUR FEAR AND STARVES YOUR FAITH.

Truth be told, the enemy is constantly trying to put your calling into question. He does this because he knows all too well that the by-product of calling is confidence.

This is why I want young people to get gripped by a sense of calling from a young age. Because to simply tell young people what not to do does not hold a whole lot of power. But when they are driven by calling, they have a confidence that supersedes any peer pressure or temporal pleasure that the enemy can throw at them to corrupt their sense of self-worth.

The apostle Paul writes about the danger of comparison. He says, "We do not dare to classify or compare ourselves with some who commend themselves. When they measure themselves by themselves and compare themselves with themselves, they are not wise" (2 Corinthians 10:12, NIV).

Now the truth is, with society's addiction to social media, we live in a culture of constant comparison that pressures you into presenting perfection and hiding reality.

While the danger of playing into comparison with others is fairly obvious, Paul takes it further and says that what is also unwise is comparing yourself with yourself. This can be a sneaky and unexpected enemy to face. While comparing yourself to others often produces a misunderstanding of self-worth or of thinking too lowly of yourself, self-comparison can result in an overestimation of yourself.

We have a picture of this in scripture with our main character Joshua. So far through this book we have been using the journey of the Israelites into the Promised Land as our case study for fighting fear, so let's again take a look at our text.

Joshua, we now know, had the task of taking the people of God into the promise. They had come up against a great opponent infamously known as Jericho. It was a fortified and walled city that had greatly intimidated the people for 40 years previously. But what we discovered was that by faith they overcame. By faith they marched, by faith they shouted, by faith they blew trumpets, and by faith the walls came down. It was on the other side of their faith that God gave the Israelites a great victory that day.

As great as that victory was, God had called them to occupy the entire land, which meant there were more enemies to face. Even as believers today, we need to keep moving forward in life. Just as the Israelites could not stay camped in Jericho, we also cannot camp in yesterday's victory. Too often we stay stuck in our ten-year-old testimony, talking about what God did way back when. While there is nothing wrong with talking about what God did in our life ten years ago, sometimes it can hold us back from taking new territory.

For the Israelites, the Promised Land was still possessed by enemies, and God still had more ground for them to take. However, because of their recent victory over Jericho, their confidence had now reached a whole new level. You could say that they felt unstoppable. No other invading force had overcome the great walled city; no other army had decimated an enemy like they had, so who could possibly stand in their way?

Check out what happens when you compare yourself with yourself:

> Joshua sent some of his men from Jericho to spy out the town of Ai, east of Beth-el, near Beth-aven. When they returned, they told Joshua, "There's no need for all of us to go up there; it won't take more than two or three thousand men to attack Ai. Since there are so few of them, don't make all our people struggle to go up there." So approximately 3,000 warriors were sent, but they were soundly defeated. The men of Ai chased the Israelites from the town gate as far as the quarries, and they killed about thirty-six who were retreating down the slope. The Israelites were paralyzed with fear at this turn of events, and their courage melted away.
>
> **(JOSHUA 7:2-5, NLT)**

The Israelites had entered the Promised Land with a truckload of insecurities and uncertainties. For generations they had been slaves in Egypt, and as a community they had forgotten their identity as the people of God. Whenever they faced off with opposition, it intimidated them because they had forgotten who God had called them to be.

But now that they had a great victory in Jericho, they failed to recognize who it was that had actually won the victory for them. They became complacent—

so much so that the very next battle they faced, they considered their ability in comparison to their recent victory.

Now, before we start judging the Israelites, we need to realize what this looks like in our life: to be victorious in one season only to struggle with the same thing in the next season. Maybe you overcame self-esteem issues in high school only to be driven by the need for approval in the workplace. Or maybe you thought you had graduated from jealousy in relationships only to struggle with trusting your spouse now that you're married.

For Joshua, he sent out the spies as he had done before and, as it had been previously, the report was optimistic, but with one major difference: The report from the spies who entered Jericho in Joshua 2:24 says, "The Lord has given us the whole land" (Joshua 2:24, NLT).

In the case of Ai, however, God was not a part of the report at all: "When they returned, they told Joshua, 'There's no need for all of us to go up there; it won't take more than two or three thousand men to attack Ai. Since there are so few of them, don't make all our people struggle to go up there'" (Joshua 7:3, NLT).

REFLECTION

In other words, it wasn't the fear the Israelites had but the fear they lacked that caused their defeat this time around. I'm talking about the kind of fear that we actually need, which is known as the fear of the Lord.

This is different from being afraid of God. I find that a lot of people walk around in life afraid that God is somehow disappointed with them and that He is simply waiting for them to trip up or make a mistake so that He can punish them. This kind of fear only comes from a poor perception of God.

Fear comes from wondering if God can, if God will, or if God would. But fearing the Lord is not a wonder if but a wonder of God.

A simple Google search will reveal over 100 scripture references in God's Word talking about the fear of the Lord. Instead of giving you a list of passages that will help develop the fear of the Lord in your life, I want to simply give you one word that holds the key to producing a deeper fear of the Lord than anything else. And that word is "reflection."

Admittedly, I'm not so great at the art of reflection. On our first church birthday, I can remember that we had broken attendance records, our new-guest ratios were off the charts, and the worship experience was spectacular. We were sitting down with some friends that evening, and I began to talk about all the things that we could do better next Sunday. Keira quietly pulled me into the kitchen and said, "Honey, can we just for a moment reflect and celebrate what God did today before we go on to the next thing?"

I realized I had not even paused to acknowledge where the victory had really come from. Reflection is what leads to gratitude, which is ultimately an acknowledgment of the fact that without God we would have none of these blessings.

This was the case for the Israelites. They failed to

reflect. They went from a victory in one area straight into another battle. As they went up against Ai, they failed to remember that it is the Lord who brings the victory—not their fighting skill, not their brilliant strategy, not their 401k or stock options, but the Lord.

The Israelites had compared themselves with themselves and considered their own strength for the task. This will only produce pride in the heart of the believer and cause you to miss God in every occasion.

The art of reflection has actually been God's design from the beginning. What we have in scripture—starting from Genesis—is a system of worship established by God that involves what is known as an altar. This is a structure upon which God's people could focus their worship, as well as to glorify God and recognize His provision, protection and providence in a way that was acceptable to Him.

An Old Testament altar was a place of sacrifice and redemption, set up as a memorial to God's provision, breakthrough and power. An altar was where the divine and human world would interact. It was a place of exchange and a place of encounter. Not only were there specific practices outlined in God's Word for what took place at or on the altar, but the very construction of an altar was also specific. Whether it was an altar built for sin sacrifice or an altar built as a memorial pillar, how the altar was built came with specific instruction as to achieve the very purpose for which it was intended.

We see an example of this in Exodus where God is speaking to Moses right after He has revealed to the people of Israel the 10 commandments: the law they were to live by in order to remain righteous as God's own people. However, God knew that the people would be unable to keep these commandments and coupled with the commandments a system of sacrifice. An animal's shed blood could atone temporarily for the sin that was committed, and therefore redeem the sinner. This very act was to take place upon an altar.

God actually gives Moses a specific description of how and when to build an altar. He said,

> Build for me an altar made of earth, and offer your sacrifices to me—your burnt offerings and peace offerings, your sheep and goats, and your cattle. Build my altar wherever I cause my name to be remembered, and I will come to you and bless you. If you use stones to build my altar, use only natural, uncut stones. Do not shape the stones with a tool, for that would make the altar unfit for holy use.
>
> **(EXODUS 20:24-25, NLT)**

God instructs Moses to build an altar made from natural uncut stones. We see this several times throughout scripture. In Genesis 28, we see that Jacob set up a stone as a pillar and poured oil over it like an altar. He named the place Bethel, meaning "house of God." We see that every time the Lord brought Abraham into a new land, Abraham built an altar in recognition of God's provision. We see that Joshua retrieved 12 stones from the Jordan River and set them up as memorial pillars or an altar to the Lord, recognizing deliverance.

These old covenant altars were a place of remembrance and reflection where sacrifices could be made. Now what started out as simple, an altar made of uncut stone, became very complicated under the system of law. As mentioned before, there were very specific sacrifices, for very specific situations. Leviticus gives us a detailed description of what offerings and sacrifices atoned for what sin. There were grain offerings, guilt offerings, sacrifices that atoned for coveting, sacrifices that atoned for stealing, and even sacrifices that were to be made for the cleansing of skin sores.

Leviticus 14 actually reveals in detail the process someone had to go through to be cleared of a skin disease. They essentially had to show themselves to the priest who would then make a series of sacrifices upon the stone altar by which they could be clean and cleared to enter back into society. We also see an example of this with Jesus in Luke 17. Here we have Jesus traveling to Jerusalem where He encounters a group of lepers:

> As Jesus continued on toward Jerusalem, he reached the border between Galilee and Samaria. As he entered a village there, ten men with leprosy stood at a distance, crying out, "Jesus, Master, have mercy on us!" He looked at them and said, "Go show yourselves to the priests." And as they went, they were cleansed of their leprosy.
>
> **(LUKE 17:11-14, NLT)**

Not only do we have an amazing miracle recorded here but also an intersection of old covenant and new covenant—a collision of the old covenant of law and the new covenant of grace that Jesus was establishing. The story records ten lepers who had been outcast from society and forced to live in isolation on the outskirts of the community. Recognizing Jesus, they cry out to Him to heal them, and Jesus does something fascinating.

He commands them to go and show themselves to the priests. He essentially employs the Levitical ordinance of being cleared by a priest as recorded under the system of law. And the Bible says that "as they went they were healed."

The passage goes on to say,

> One of them, when he saw that he was healed, came back to Jesus, shouting, "Praise God!" He fell to the ground at Jesus' feet, thanking him for what he had done. This man was a Samaritan. Jesus asked, "Didn't I heal ten men? Where are the other nine? Has no one returned to give glory to God except this foreigner?" And Jesus said to the man, "Stand up and go. Your faith has healed you."
> **(LUKE 17:15-19, NLT)**

Here we have ten men, nine of whom were Jews and one a Samaritan. Now Jews and Samaritans never mixed in ordinary circumstances, but in life you will discover that misery loves company! So we have this mixed bag of lepers living in isolation. Upon realizing that they were healed, only the Samaritan (just one out of the ten—a tithe!) returned to Jesus full of thankfulness. And Jesus asks a confronting question. He says, "Didn't I heal ten men? Where are the other nine? Has no one returned to give glory to God except this foreigner?"

What makes this question confronting is the fact that the Samaritan did not return to Jesus after seeing the priest but "upon seeing that he was healed." So Jesus essentially knew where the other nine men were. They were going to see the priest as He had commanded. But what is easy to miss in this interaction is actually what Jesus was ultimately doing. Jesus was revealing how to build a new covenant altar.

You see, an old covenant altar was an uncut stone upon which a sacrifice would be made by a priest. It involved a lengthy and repetitive process. But in 1 Peter 2, we see Peter give a unique description of Jesus:

> As you come to him, the living Stone—rejected by men but chosen by God and precious to him—you also, like living stones, are being built into a spiritual house to be a holy priesthood, offering spiritual sacrifices acceptable to God through Jesus Christ.
>
> **(1 PETER 2:4-5, NIV)**

The purpose of an old covenant altar, an uncut stone, was to facilitate the process of being declared clean. Jesus here was revealing Himself as the living stone, who would be the sacrifice declaring once and for all holy. We no longer need a priest as an intermediary, but we are being built into a holy priesthood ourselves. You see, while the nine went to the priest, the Samaritan became a priest by making his altar at the feet of Jesus through thankfulness.

What is the new covenant altar? Well, the writer

of Hebrews says, "Through Jesus, therefore, let us continually offer to God a sacrifice of praise—the fruit of lips that confess his name. And do no forget to do good and to share with others, for with such sacrifices God is pleased" (Hebrews 13:15-16, NIV).

This is how we build a new covenant altar—with praise—no longer of stone, but in our hearts with thankfulness and remembrance. In fact, we come to the altar to alter our perspective and to align our purpose. A proper appropriation of reflection in our life will produce the kind of humility that will allow you to boast properly.

That's right, God does want us to learn how to boast—properly that is.

RESPONSE

What do I mean? Well, Paul includes in his letter to the Corinthians not just a warning against comparison but also instructions about the best way to boast. He says, "We, however, will not boast beyond proper limits, but will confine our boasting to the sphere of service God himself has assigned to us, a sphere that also includes you" (2 Corinthians 10:13, NIV).

The apostle instructs us to essentially not compare ourselves with others or even ourselves but to keep our comparison to Christ and His power at work in our lives. It is only when you compare your limited resources with Christ's unlimited power that a platform is produced for God's miraculous power.

Paul essentially says, "So you're gonna see me boast, but it's not me I'm boasting about. I'm going to boast in the Lord!" This is how we are meant to compare—comparing our limitations with how great and mighty and marvelous and wonderful and majestic our LORD is: "O LORD, our Lord, How majestic is Your name in all the earth!" (Psalm 8:9, NIV).

But how do I not boast beyond proper limits? What is the gauge to know when I'm moving from boasting in what the Lord has done in my life, also known as a testimony or giving glory to God, and simply bragging about me?

I believe the key is in being self-aware. This topic can be tricky waters to navigate because, as a pastor, I want so badly for people to have a healthy self-image with the kind of self-confidence that will produce bold action. Yet, at the same time, I know that there is a tipping point where a good self-image can move into an inflated ego. So how are we meant to know the proper limits?

Let me suggest that it starts and ends with our understanding of grace, which is the undeserved and unmerited favor of God. The fact that God chose me and continues to choose me despite my inadequacies, flaws and failings is reason enough to be humbled and restrained in my boasting about me.

Throughout Paul's ministry, he carried the awareness of grace. He knew full well that at the point grace entered his life, he was literally opposing the work of God. So in his estimation of himself, he realized that he brought nothing to the table except an empty vessel that God could fill. But this is no reason to see yourself as worthless. Even an empty vessel has value if the contents within it are of great worth. This is how we become self-aware: aware of who we are and what it is that we carry. As a carrier of the presence of God and the message of hope, we give God greater glory because of our weaknesses. The Bible refers to us as "earthen vessels": "But we have this treasure in earthen vessels, that the excellency of the power may be of God, and not of us" (2 Corinthians 4:7, KJV).

I love this image because there is nothing impressive about a clay jar. It's fragile, it's bland, and it's very common. What you place within that clay jar is what determines its worth.

This understanding is what frames our response to God and what He has done for us. This is why I respond with gratitude and thankfulness, because I am all too aware of what I carry within me and what it really is that makes me valuable.

day seven

COMPARISON VS INSPIRATION

"Comparison feeds your fear and starves your faith."

Yesterday we learned that our words create the world around us. We were made in the image of God with the capacity to create a life in line with the calling that God has placed on our lives—lives of faith. But doing so is much easier said than done. Instead of creating a life that is unique to our purpose, we often find ourselves comparing to those around us and modeling our own lives by what they have created.

In fact, a lot of supposed inspiration is just mislabeled comparison. In the table below, identify which motivations come from comparison versus creativity from God in your world.

Where my inspiration comes from...

COMPARISON ex. copying	CREATIVITY ex. pioneering

The problem with comparison is that God has created us all with our own individual calling. He is even aware of the areas we are weak. Rather than evaluating our weaknesses and comparing them to others or considering ourselves more capable than we are, God wants us to employ our weaknesses to see His strength through the right filter—not through comparison or through pride—but understanding that limitations can be leverage when compared with the greatness of God.

What areas in your life have you seen as weak that actually reveal God's strength?

_____

_____

_____

_____

_____

_____

_____

_____

_____

_____

day eight

THE ART OF REFLECTION

"Reflection is what leads to gratitude, which is ultimately an acknowledgment of the fact that without God we would have none of these blessings."

A New Testament altar is a place to align our purpose and perspective with the will of God by presenting our praise as a sacrifice to God. Hebrews 13:15 (NIV) tells us that we should "continually offer to God a sacrifice of praise—the fruit of lips that confess his name."

But in order to offer praises to God for all He has done, we must first have an accurate picture of the ways that He has transformed us. This is the art of reflection: learning to take the time to catalogue all that God has done in your past so that you will have faith for all He will do in the future.

Think specifically over the last 2 years in your life and document two ways that God has transformed you during that time period. What are you grateful for that God has done?

_____

_____

_____

_____

_____

_____

_____

_____

_____

_____

_____

_____

_____

_____

_____

What are you believing for God to do in the next 2 years?

_____

_____

_____

_____

_____

_____

_____

_____

_____

_____

_____

_____

_____

The Bible says that even "[i]f we are unfaithful, he remains faithful, for he cannot deny who he is" (2 Timothy 2:13, NLT).

How does God's faithfulness in the past affect the faith you have for your vision of the future?

_____

_____

_____

_____

_____

_____

_____

_____

_____

_____

_____

_____

day nine

FEAR OF THE LORD

"It is only when you compare your limited resources with Christ's unlimited power that a platform is produced for God's miraculous power."

Pride is dangerous. The Word of God says that "pride goes before destruction, and haughtiness before a fall" (Proverbs 16:18, NLT). When we consider ourselves better than we are, we run the risk of making the same mistake the devil made—desiring praise for ourselves rather than for praise to run through us to its rightful place with God.

Even though we are meant to be humble, we are not meant to have deflated self-esteem. Instead, God wants us to have a healthy understanding of His grace—the undeserved and unmerited favor of God. When you fully comprehend that, despite your failings, God has chosen you and saved you, then you are humbled to His awesome power at work in your life.

You don't see yourself as deficient; you just hold a healthy understanding of grace that will lead you to keep coming back to God for His love, His wisdom, and His forgiveness.

Think critically about your prayer life: are there areas that you never bring to God due to pride that you can handle it all on your own?

"Fear of the LORD is the foundation of wisdom. Knowledge of the Holy One results in good judgment" (Proverbs 9:10, NLT). As we've learned from Joshua and the Israelites' defeat at Ai, boasting in our own strength can lead us to make decisions that ultimately bring defeat. Yet when we have the right kind of fear—the fear of the Lord—then we are in the position to make good decisions that keep us in line with His will and lead to victory.

After reading this section, what is your understanding of walking in the fear of God?

_____

_____

_____

_____

_____

_____

_____

_____

_____

_____

_____

_____

_____

_____

_____

_____

_____

_____

_____

_____

_____

_____

_____

_____

_____

_____

_____

_____

4

HANDLING FEAR

When Israel had finished killing all the men of Ai in the fields
and in the desert where they had chased them,
and when every one of them had been put to the sword,
all the Israelites returned to Ai and killed those who were in it.
Twelve thousand men and women fell that
day—all the people of Ai.
For Joshua did not draw back the hand that
held out his javelin
until he had destroyed all who lived in Ai.

JOSHUA 8:24-26 (NIV)

Have you ever been slightly impressed with yourself? Be honest: surely there has been at least some time in your life where you thought, *Hey! I did pretty well!*

In my first-ever paid ministry position, I was hired as the youth pastor. At the time I was an electrician and a volunteer youth leader in a small church and had been invited to speak at a citywide youth conference.

There were a number of churches represented, which made for a supercharged event. The atmosphere was charged, the worship was electric, and the energy from the young people was wild. I cannot exactly recall what sermon I preached, but I do remember preaching so hard that I sweat through both of the T-shirts I was wearing.

After the session, a very well known pastor approached me and said, "Good job tonight. Why don't you come in for a chat this week?" He was the lead pastor of the largest church in our city, so I was excited about the invitation. Little did I know that it would be a surprise interview.

Needless to say, the conversation went well, and I was offered the position at the church as the full-time youth pastor. Back in those days, however, when you were hired on as the youth pastor your first duty was to preach that very Sunday. I had spoken at a bunch of youth events, high schools and camps, but that was to young people. They were fun and forgiving. Speaking in front of adults in the largest church in our city was a terrifying idea. I was freaking out and wondering why I even agreed to this job. At the same time, I knew that if God had called me, then I had to act confident. Even if I was

was not confident, I was going to pretend.

I preached my heart out and made sure no one could tell that I was nervous, even though I was totally terrified. To my relief it went well, and the church loved it. But that week I had a one-on-one with my pastor, my new boss, who for some reason I expected to applaud my efforts. He asked me, "How do you think you did?"

To which I replied honestly, "Really good actually. What did you think?"

To my surprise, he said, "Not bad, but you really need to work on your arrogance!"

I was shocked. That was not what I was expecting to hear at all. I mean, I was freaking out and was not over-confident. I was ready to quit in the first week on the job. I went home to tell Keira what had happened and said, "Babe, I'm done. I don't need this." I knew she'd be with me; we were like Bonnie and Clyde, and she was my ride or die. I knew she would be just as offended at his comment and assessment.

However, she looked at me and said, "Well, maybe he's right." She said that there's a big difference between being humble and pretending.

I realized that day that fear loves to disguise itself as humility.

We find in Paul the apostle's letter to the church in Corinth that this was his situation. He was writing in defense of his apostleship against a group of self-proclaimed and self-ordained super-apostles who possessed incredible ability but zero humility. He says, "For it is not the one who commends himself who is approved, but the one whom the Lord commends"

(2 Corinthians 10:18, NIV).

In other words, Paul wants to develop a church that experiences victory, yet at the same time models humility. As a believer, it is vitally important to understand that while we are victorious in this life, it does not mean that we do not ever experience defeat. It can be confusing to those who are new to faith to find that God calls us more than conquerors, but we still face battles we cannot seem to win. What is powerful is when you mature in your walk with God to the place where you realize that God can do just as much with defeat as He can with victory. For instance, defeat can certainly develop into despair, but it can also produce a deeper dependency on God. This is the ultimate goal of the Christian life: not independence from God but a greater dependence with every step.

> "THIS IS THE ULTIMATE GOAL OF THE CHRISTIAN LIFE: NOT INDEPENDENCE FROM GOD BUT A GREATER DEPENDENCE WITH EVERY STEP.

While Paul was addressing this group of influencers that were infiltrating the church, he also used this teaching to target the entire church. He says,

> We, however, will not boast beyond proper limits, but will confine our boasting to the sphere of service God himself has assigned to us, a sphere that also includes you. We are not going too far in our boasting, as would be the case if we had not

come to you, for we did get as far as you with the gospel of Christ. Neither do we go beyond our limits by boasting of work done by others. Our hope is that, as your faith continues to grow, our sphere of activity among you will greatly expand, so that we can preach the gospel in the regions beyond you. For we do not want to boast about work already done in someone else's territory. But, "Let the one who boasts boast in the Lord.

(2 CORINTHIANS 10:13-17, NIV)

Paul is not suggesting that we do not praise people in case they become prideful. By all means, encourage each other. No, Paul is talking about those who commend themselves.

But those who disqualify themselves can be just as destructive as those who boast in themselves. Because of circumstance, attitudes and environments, the most destructive thing to God's plan for you could be you and your very own disqualification of yourself.

I love the way the Bible is written, because time and time again we see the invitation to "take courage" or "take heart," as if to indicate that at any given time or moment in life what is available to us is both faith and fear—almost like the choice is yours. In any given situation or circumstance, you can choose fear or you can take faith. The problem I think we all find is facing situations where the fear is so overwhelming that no matter how hard we try we cannot find the faith option.

I'm talking about holding on to faith when you're out of work and your rent is past due. I'm talking about holding on to faith when your child is sick and has been hospitalized. I'm talking about holding on to faith in the midst of fearful situations.

So how do we hold on to faith when the fear is too much to handle?

Well, our main guy Joshua had some experience with this very situation. As we discovered in the previous chapters, Joshua and the Israelites journey through the unknown Promised Land. While we may have marched by faith around Jericho experiencing a great victory, we have also felt the sting of defeat at Ai. Now we find Joshua with the task of finding the faith needed to lead the nation to fight again. Check it out:

> Then the Lord said to Joshua, "Do not be afraid; do not be discouraged. Take the whole army with you, and go up and attack Ai. For I have delivered into your hands the king of Ai, his people, his city and his land. You shall do to Ai and its king as you did to Jericho and its king, except that you may carry off their plunder and livestock for yourselves. Set an ambush behind the city."
>
> **(JOSHUA 8:1-2, NIV)**

Here we have the Lord God commanding Joshua to not be discouraged. God informs Joshua that He has already delivered into his hands the very opponent that just defeated them. It is essentially the same thing that God said to Joshua when they faced the wall of Jericho. He said to Joshua, "See, I have given you the city." Even though what is standing between Joshua and that city is a heavily fortified wall, God says, "It's yours." This is what can be most confusing in the life of the believer—when what you see in front of you and in your life doesn't look like what God said about your life.

And so Joshua, still discouraged and defeated, receives a command from God combined with a strategy: to "go up against the enemy again, but this time . . . take all your men . . ." Now let me pause for a moment to make one thing clear. With any victory in our life, it's certainly God who brings the victory. In fact, it's *all* Him. Yet, while God gives the victory, He's not interested in anything less than our full participation!

If we were to take some time and break down the strategy that God gives Joshua, we would see that God is now trapping the enemy with the same trap the enemy used to gain victory over God's people! This is how God wants to work in your world. He wants to take the very areas of addiction that used to have a hold on you, the areas in your life where you find that you are weak, and develop a testimony that holds the power to set people free through placing His strength over your weaknesses.

We see this displayed in Joshua's first defeat as leader. All the confidence he had gained coming off the Jericho victory was now in question. However, God instructs Joshua to take the enemy on again. Joshua, despite being afraid of the enemy, *has an even greater fear of the Lord* and does as the Lord instructs. This time, he seeks God for strategy and sets an ambush in place using some of his men as bait to entice all the fighting men out of the city.

Let's read what it says in verse 18:

Then the Lord said to Joshua, "Hold out toward
Ai the javelin that is in your hand, for into your hand
I will deliver the city." So Joshua held out his javelin
toward Ai.

(JOSHUA 8:18, NIV)

Now this is a key instruction that the Lord gives to
Joshua. Up until recently he had been an apprentice
under Moses. Something we have not given due credit
to over this book is the role of Moses in Joshua's world.
I mean, as we have been following the triumphs of
Joshua, we easily compare them with where Moses
failed or how he learned from Moses' mistakes.

But I have discovered that it is one thing to follow
someone's example and learn from their mistakes
and another thing to be the one to pioneer the
path with no bearing on where you are going or
experience to draw from. And so maybe we could
take a moment to consider Moses, because Moses
also had to handle his own fear.

WHAT'S IN YOUR HAND?

In Exodus 3, we see God speak to Moses through
the burning bush. And God reveals to Moses that He
has heard the cry of His people and has called Moses
to lead the people out of captivity. The only problem
is that Moses is afraid, even after God told him what
will happen and what to say.

What if they do not believe me or listen to me
and say, "The Lord did not appear to you"? Then
the Lord said to him, "What is that in your hand?"

(EXODUS 4:1-2, NIV)

All that Moses had was a staff, which God commanded him to throw on the ground. As soon as Moses released it, the staff turned into a snake. While in Moses' hand, it was a simple staff. Once released from his hand, it released the very power of God.

Again we see another story in Exodus 17 with a battle between the Israelites and the Amalekites. At this time, Moses is leading the nation, and Joshua is the military leader fighting a difficult battle. While Joshua was on the battlefield amidst the dust, the clashing of swords, and the battle cries, Moses stood on top of a nearby hill with his staff held out before God. Joshua, in the thick of the conflict, noticed a swelling tide of victory and then defeat. He realized that whenever Moses held out the staff, they were victorious, but whenever Moses grew tired and the staff dropped, the enemy gained the advantage.

Now hold that thought for a minute as we fast-forward to the battle Joshua is facing as the new leader of Israel.

His opponent is an enemy who had previously defeated them, and yet God reminds him of a strategy that he had previously experienced: an unconventional strategy that involved a staff.

Now we have Joshua, who is standing in a battle with a staff of sorts; the Bible describes it as a weapon, a javelin, also known as a spear. But what God was wanting to reveal to Joshua was that the weapon itself was not going to win the victory. God was going to give it into their hand! "Do not be afraid or discouraged because of this vast army. For the battle is not yours, but God's" (2 Chronicles 20:15, NIV).

For God to give into Joshua's hand what was in God's hand, Joshua first had to hold out what was in his hand.

Maybe in your life this could look like a financial battle that is too much to handle, but you've been trying to handle it. I need to remind you that the battle is the Lord's. He simply asks you to hold out what's in your hand.

This is how the tithe has an effect in your life. About a year ago I spoke to someone who had started tithing but gave up after one month. They said, "It didn't work, and you said that we can test God in this. Well, He failed." What they failed to realize is that God is looking for faithfulness. He's looking for you to not just lift your hand, but keep holding out your hand until you have seen the victory.

There are certainly seasons when you will face circumstances that produce fear: death of a loved one, loss of a job, unfavorable diagnosis, broken relationships. These battles make it hard to "switch on faith."

It was the lead pastor who first hired me as a youth pastor who taught me so much about faith. Under his ministry I experienced a faith-filled leader who led with boldness and determination time and time again. He was a great leader.

But what was surprising to me was to receive a call from him years later where he shared with me that he had suffered a severe burnout. Ministry fatigue came from a series of struggles and disappointments, leaving him lacking the energy to fight. It was during that call when this model of faith told me that he knew that all he had to do in that season was switch on faith, but he simply could not find the switch. He said it was like feeling around in a dark room at night, knowing that there was a switch somewhere but not being able to find it.

I asked him how he got through that season, to which he said, "One day at a time, and one battle at a time. I had to fight what was in front of me." He went on to tell me that it meant that he kept taking phone calls, he kept turning up to church, and he kept reading the Word.

What I discovered from this experience was that in the seasons when you can't seem to be faith filled, you simply need to be faithful with what you have, knowing that you have a God who is faithful.

"WHEN YOU CAN'T SEEM TO BE FAITH FILLED, YOU SIMPLY NEED TO BE FAITHFUL WITH WHAT YOU HAVE.

You see, just as the Israelites are about to attack the enemy, the Lord reminds Joshua of a time when he was in battle and looked up on the hillside and saw Moses holding out his staff. Joshua remembered that as long as Moses was faithful to hold out what was in his hand, then they were victorious.

And now God gives the same instruction to Joshua. It reminded him that he had been here before:

When Israel had finished killing all the men of Ai in the fields and in the desert where they had chased them, and when every one of them had been put to the sword, all the Israelites returned to Ai and killed those who were in it. Twelve thousand men and women fell that day—all the people of Ai. For Joshua did not draw back the hand that held out his javelin until he had destroyed all who lived in Ai.

(JOSHUA 8:24-26, NIV)

Joshua did not draw back his hand. Joshua's leadership in this battle was not one of courageous faith, it was simply one of consistent faith, otherwise known as staying faithful.

But maybe that is where things get difficult, because you realize that there has not been much faithfulness on your part. Well, Paul has some good news for you. As he shared with Timothy, "If we are unfaithful, he remains faithful, for he cannot deny who he is" (2 Timothy 2:13, NLT).

God's faithfulness is a constant theme throughout scripture. You see, it was a faithful God who in Genesis did not give up on Adam and Eve, even though they rebelled against His command. It was a faithful God who was faithful to Noah, even though the whole nation sinned and turned from Him. It was a faithful God who was faithful to Abraham, even though he doubted his ability to fulfill what God had promised. It was a faithful God who was faithful to Sarah, who laughed in contempt at the promise of God.

Now that I know what's in my hand, talking about the ability to be faithful with what I have, I'm positioned to get some wins in my world.

WHERE CAN WE WIN?

The reason fear is effective in keeping the believer immobilized is that fear's counterpart is failure. Failure, like comparison, will feed our fear and starve our faith. Failure, disappointment and defeat will always give way to fear and will begin to infiltrate all areas of our life like a noxious weed. Failure perpetuates even more failure, producing a negative momentum that, left unattended or unaddressed, will produce a timid life.

But as the apostle Paul said to Timothy in his second letter, "For God has not given us a spirit of fear but of power, of love and of a sound mind" (2 Timothy 1:17, NKJV).

The best way to combat failure and arrest the momentum it perpetuates in my life is to get a win—somewhere. Knowing I have a spirit of power is exciting, and knowing I have a spirit of love is comforting, but the fact that I have a sound mind means I can be more strategic than surprised by what happens in life.

What if in the midst of failures I could turn even my worst days into a win? It's difficult to change our circumstances and the situations we find ourselves in. But what if I could change the way I see those circumstances? You see, even pain holds power if there is purpose to it. I might not enjoy painful things—who does?—but if there is purpose to the pain, then, while I don't enjoy it, I may be able to endure it.

This is the same with lack and limitation. When I stay fixated on what I do not have or what I need, then I feel like a failure. But when I allow God to use my need to meet a need in someone else, then even my needs cause me to win.

We see this with Elijah in 1 Kings. The nation was in a famine, yet God had been supplying for the prophet's needs with a brook and some ravens. Then one day the brook dried up and the ravens stopped delivering food—creating a need in Elijah's life. Instead of staying stuck in his need, the prophet allowed that need to direct him to the widow of Zarephath who was in desperate need of a miracle.

I dare say that despite any sudden change of circumstance in your life for the better, God can still cause you to win right where you are; it simply requires you to reframe where you find the win.

We recently enrolled our twins, Zali and Zara, in our local public middle school. Now any parent knows that this is a terrifying process simply because we can still remember the sting of rejection and the awkward interactions we had at that time. However, what comforted us in this unnerving process was the discovery that our new middle school principal was actually a believer who previously worked as a school campus youth minister. Upon meeting him and through conversation, he revealed that even though he enjoyed his role as a youth minister, it was a painful experience for him and his wife. After several years of doing their best to make it work, they experienced near financial ruin and both ended up applying for a teaching position out of sheer desperation. Little did they know that it would begin an accelerated journey to being the principal of the very school he attended as a kid himself. Not only that, he says that now he is having a far greater influence and impact for the kingdom in the lives of students and families than he ever did as a school youth minister. I found one revelation of his particularly amazing. He said, "At the time of being forced to quit our youth ministry roles, we were frustrated and confused. But now we see so clearly that, if it had not been for that terrible circumstance, we wouldn't be where we are now! Funny how God works."

This is a great example of where we can win. Even in the midst of loss, hardship, and confusing situations, God is working all things together for an outcome we could not even predict. Go through enough of these kinds of situations in life, and you will begin to see faith through a different lens.

Now, if we have established that failure isn't a limiter to faith, what about foolishness? In the next chapter we will discover what makes our mistakes and what our mistakes can also make.

WHAT'S IN YOUR HAND?

"This is the ultimate goal of the Christian life: not independence from God but a greater dependence with every step."

God has designed us for relationship with Him. As believers, we can regularly fall into two camps:

1. Those who pride themselves on their ability—taking what God has given us and trying to put it work for ourselves, or

2. Those who disqualify ourselves because we know that we feel like we don't have the skills, gifts, or circumstances needed to achieve the call of God on our lives.

In both attitudes, we forget to consider how God can factor into the equation. God is always the source of our strength; if we are constantly returning to Him for guidance, then we can be assured that our pride will not lead us to destruction. At the same time, God's strength is so clear in our weakness. Instead of over-qualifying ourselves or disqualifying ourselves, the goal should be to surrender what we have been given to God. For Joshua, he holds out his javelin towards the people of Ai. As he does so, his people see victory.

God has placed things in your hand—or control—as well.

What's currently in your hand that you can hold out to God? In other words, what areas do you know you need to surrender?

_____

_____

_____

_____

_____

_____

_____

_____

_____

_____

_____

_____

When you cannot seem to be faith filled, you simply need to be faithful with what you have, knowing you have a God who is faithful.

In what ways can you be faithful with what God has already given you?

_____

_____

_____

_____

_____

_____

_____

_____

_____

_____

_____

_____

_____

_____

_____

_____

_____

_____

_____

_____

_____

_____

_____

_____

_____

_____

_____

_____

day eleven

WHERE CAN WE WIN?

"Even in the midst of loss, hardship, and confusing situations, God is working all things together for an outcome we could not even predict."

Sometimes life can be confusing when we are told that we are victorious but then encounter real defeats in our lives. If we are not careful, failure can lead you to become passive in your approach—starving faith the same way that comparison does.

The Bible says, "God causes everything to work together for the good of those who love God and are called according to his purpose for them" (Romans 8:28, NLT). It doesn't say just some things. It says that God causes EVERYTHING to work together for your good. Isn't that incredible?

That means that no matter what is happening in your world, there is a win you can find within the challenge. It is all a matter of perspective.

Read the following stories in the Bible and highlight the ways that God worked things together for good:

- Genesis 6-9: Noah's story
- Genesis 37-45: Joseph's story
- John 11: Lazarus's story

With these examples in mind, how can you reframe where you find the win in your life today?

_____

_____

_____

_____

_____

_____

_____

_____

_____

_____

_____

_____

_____

_____

_____

_____

5

WHAT'S FAITH AND
WHAT'S FOOLISH

But when the people of Gibeon heard what Joshua had
done
to Jericho and Ai, they resorted to deception to save
themselves.
They sent ambassadors to Joshua, loading their donkeys
with weathered saddlebags and old, patched wineskins.
They put on worn-out, patched sandals and ragged clothes.
And the bread they took with them was dry and moldy.
When they arrived at the camp of Israel at Gilgal,
they told Joshua and the men of Israel,
"We have come from a distant land to ask you to make a
peace treaty with us."
The Israelites replied to these Hivites, "How do we know you
don't live nearby?
For if you do, we cannot make a treaty with you."
They replied, "We are your servants."
"But who are you?" Joshua demanded. "Where do you
come from?"
They answered, "Your servants have come from a very
distant country. We have heard of the might of the Lord your
God and of all he did in Egypt.
(We have also heard what he did to the two Amorite kings
east of the Jordan River—)
So our elders and all our people instructed us, 'Take supplies
for a long journey.
Go meet with the people of Israel and tell them,

"We are your servants; please make a treaty with us."'
"This bread was hot from the ovens when we left our homes.
But now, as you can see, it is dry and moldy.
These wineskins were new when we filled them, but now they
are old and split open.
And our clothing and sandals are worn out from our very
long journey."
So the Israelites examined their food, but they did not consult
the Lord.
Then Joshua made a peace treaty with them and
guaranteed their safety, and the leaders of the community
ratified their agreement with a binding oath.

JOSHUA 9:3-14 (NLT)

Like almost all children, my daughters love bedtime stories.

However, they are never interested in stories read from a book; they always want to hear stories of when I was young and the crazy things I got up to as a kid. What is most disturbing is that they only ever want to hear stories where I was either hurt, humiliated, or did something stupid.

Fortunately for them, I have an ample supply, and most of them center around my wife, Keira. This is no surprise as the day that I met Keira was the day I came completely undone!

Call it what you will—lack of finesse or having no game—but as far as I was concerned, I was prepared to do whatever it took to impress this girl. As I have explained time and time again to my daughters, while I may have certainly seemed like a fool to them, it was for good reason. At that time there were many other, how do I say this, rivals—other guys who were also interested in impressing Keira, guys way smoother than me, that's for sure.

Now I was more than okay with looking like a fool if it meant that Keira didn't get fooled into believing one of those guys would be better for her than me. That's because there's a big difference between being a fool and being fooled.

Throughout this book we have been referencing Paul's letter to the church in Corinth. In fact, one of the things we are blessed to have in scripture is a series of letters from the apostle, who in my opinion was easily one of the greatest thinkers of all time. Not only does he have a unique ability to articulate kingdom principles and expound on biblical concepts, but he could even take on Greek philosophers and beat them at their own game. While others would rant with philosophical rhetoric, Paul reasoned through real experience.

In the epistles are Paul's responses to real questions, concerns and specific circumstances that were facing the church at that time. Through the Bible, we can see that the obstacles the early church faced are actually similar to the pressures the church still faces today, which is very helpful to know. That then means the very tools they needed to successfully navigate life 2,000 years ago are still the same tools we still need today.

For instance, Paul had to deal with haters—maybe not online through social media or in the same way we do, but make no mistake, Paul certainly had haters. In his letter to the Corinthians, we find him confronting a group of influencers who he considered to be false apostles. These people were opposing and undoing the good work he had begun. So, in a unique approach to pastoring, we find Paul gets, well, foolish. He says, "I hope you will put up with a little more of my foolishness. Please bear with me. For I am jealous for you with the jealousy of God himself. I promised you as a pure bride to one husband—Christ" (2 Corinthians 11:1-2, NLT).

In other words, these haters were working hard to make Paul look bad. As a result, he requests that the church bear with him in "being a fool" so that he can save them from being fooled.

This is a bold and unorthodox approach, but Paul employs it for a very good reason. Paul knew that fear will not only immobilize the church, but that fear also comes in many forms. So far, we have been identifying the different forms of fear through both the letter we have from Paul and what we see in scripture from the life of Joshua.

Essentially we've looked at faux fears, we've identified real fears, we've revealed the fear we need, and we've even explored the fear-to-faith switch. But now we find that Paul gets personal and places his own life on display by revealing his fear.

Paul puts it this way:

> But I fear that somehow your pure and undivided devotion to Christ will be corrupted, just as Eve was deceived by the cunning ways of the serpent. You happily put up with whatever anyone tells you, even if they preach a different Jesus than the one we preach, or a different kind of Spirit than the one you received, or a different kind of gospel than the one you believed.
>
> **(2 CORINTHIANS 11:3-4, NLT)**

The truth is that Paul isn't playing when it comes to the church being played. This seemingly fearless apostle, who faced all kinds of personal persecution, pressure and even pain for the advancement of the gospel, first reveals his fear and then appeals to our attention when it comes to the area of deception.

Have you ever been straight up played?

I certainly have. In 2013, just one year after we started the church, we finally moved into a real office space. As a staff team, we had been working out of our living room. While it was a convenient commute for me, it was inconvenient for family time.

I remember one Friday evening at around 6 pm the team were all still working hard, and I noticed my girls were quietly watching television, trying not to disturb the team's concentration. Seeing them confined in their own home and feeling a little guilty about it, I decided to be a good dad and take them out for a treat. I yelled out to them, "Who would like to go get pizza?"

"Me!" they at once responded excitedly. Unfortunately, so did the entire staff. The very next week I rented our first office space.

As I was working in the new space one day, a man came in asking to speak to a pastor. I invited him in and listened intently as he shared his tragic story of hardship and desperate need for assistance. I was moved with compassion, and though we did not have anything formal set up for this kind of thing, I offered him what cash I had on me on the promise of repayment when he came to church that Sunday.

Now to tell you that I have never seen that man or the money since is not surprising I'm sure, but being looped into an email from several pastors in the area warning of a fraudster matching his description turning up asking for money with a sad sob story was kind of embarrassing. I got played.

This is exactly what Paul was afraid of—not for himself, but for the church. He was afraid that they would be easily deceived, played, duped, or hoodwinked into following these false teachers. He was concerned that the foundation he had laid would somehow become corrupted, as he knew that conflicted thinking can all too easily develop into corrupted believing.

So what's the big deal? What's so bad about being fooled? Well, this is exactly how the enemy works in your life. The devil knows he cannot defeat you, simply because you are already victorious as a result of what Christ did. Instead of defeating you, he tries to distract you and ultimately render you ineffective for the kingdom. Heaven's entrance is not the goal of the Christian life. It is certainly a byproduct and benefit of a life with Christ, but it's not the goal. That's why as Christians we don't hunker down and nervously hold on tight until Jesus returns, hoping that we somehow make it.

No, the purpose of the Christian life is influence and effectiveness. This is the very reason Jesus commissioned the disciples and us to take the gospel into all the world. So, the enemy's number-one aim is to bring confusion around your calling. If he can do that, he can divert your focus off Christ and off your mission.

But Paul also knew that two can play that game.

He states to the Corinthians that there were those who were preaching a "different Jesus" than the one he preached. At the time of this letter, the name "Jesus" was a common name in the Middle East. Yet, Paul was not suggesting that they were talking about the Jesus who ran a falafel cart down the street.

Paul knew the false apostles were referring to the same Jesus that Paul preached, but they were painting Him in a different light. The false prophets were preaching about the same person but from an incorrect interpretation of Jesus that was not congruent with the facts of Jesus' life and death.

You see, they were revealing only the perfect nature or the divinity of Christ without the humanity.

And at first this seems right.

But Paul preached Christ crucified—in weakness.

These false teachers were presenting a Jesus who did not suffer or who was not humiliated and a gospel that promoted self-boasting. Their doctrine was self-seeking instead of self-denying. Their gospel glorified in themselves, commended themselves, and boasted in themselves.

Paul saw a grave mistake with this, because the premise of the gospel Paul preached was this: "I have been crucified with Christ and I no longer live, but Christ lives in me" (Galatians 2:20, NIV), and "For from him and through him and to him are all things" (Romans 11:36, NIV).

Paul did not preach that "Christ can do all things through me." He preached, "I can do all things through Christ"—not elevating his own ability, but illuminating an ever-deepening dependence on Christ.

In fact, the enemy has been trying to work this angle since the beginning of time. Ever since the garden, he has been trying to divide our devotion to Christ through his tool called deception. We see in Genesis 2 that the Lord tells Adam and Eve that they are free to eat from any tree in the garden, but there is one tree that if they eat from it they will die.

We then see in the next chapter it says, "Now the serpent was more crafty than any of the wild animals the Lord God had made. He said to the woman, 'Did God really say, 'You must not eat from any tree in the garden?''" (Genesis 3:1, NIV).

The truth is that God told them clearly they could eat from any tree but one. And so the enemy fooled Eve and rephrased the question in order to create some division in her devotion.

Let me show you another example of deception in the Bible, and of course it takes place with Joshua and the Israelites.

We have seen the enemy try to stop God's people with walls at Jericho and weapons at Ai, but what we are about to see is exactly what the enemy resorts to when he realizes he can't defeat us.

Joshua's victories were being heard about throughout the Promised Land. The Bible tells us that all the kings occupying the regions within the land were now terrified of the Israelites after hearing reports about what took place at Jericho and Ai. You have the Hittites, the Amorites, the Canaanites, the Perizzites and the Jebusites forming an alliance to fight against the Israelites.

But one group was craftier than all the other kings in the land. Knowing they could not defeat the people of God, the Gibeonites resort to another tactic:

> But when the people of Gibeon heard what Joshua had done to Jericho and Ai, they resorted to deception to save themselves. They sent ambassadors to Joshua, loading their donkeys with weathered saddlebags and old, patched wineskins. They put on worn-out, patched sandals and ragged clothes. And the bread they took with them was dry and moldy. When they arrived at the camp of Israel at Gilgal, they told Joshua and the men of Israel, "We have come from a distant land

to ask you to make a peace treaty with us." The Israelites replied to these Hivites, "How do we know you don't live nearby? For if you do, we cannot make a treaty with you." They replied, "We are your servants." "But who are you?" Joshua demanded. "Where do you come from?" They answered, "Your servants have come from a very distant country. We have heard of the might of the Lord your God and of all he did in Egypt. (We have also heard what he did to the two Amorite kings east of the Jordan River—) So our elders and all our people instructed us, 'Take supplies for a long journey. Go meet with the people of Israel and tell them, "We are your servants; please make a treaty with us.' This bread was hot from the ovens when we left our homes. But now, as you can see, it is dry and moldy. These wineskins were new when we filled them, but now they are old and split open. And our clothing and sandals are worn out from our very long journey." So the Israelites examined their food, but they did not consult the Lord. Then Joshua made a peace treaty with them and guaranteed their safety, and the leaders of the community ratified their agreement with a binding oath.

(JOSHUA 9:3-14, NLT)

We have to acknowledge the masterful play of deception by Joshua's enemies, who knew they could not defeat the people of God. Joshua took the bait of their elaborate scheme of moldy bread and was in turn fooled into an alliance with the very enemy the Israelites were meant to eradicate.

When God first told Joshua to enter the Promised

Land, God gave him clear instructions to not make a treaty with anyone living in the land, knowing full well that whatever we leave unaddressed in our life will be the very doorway for the enemy. This often happens after we come to know Christ for the first time. When we fail to submit fully to God or when we keep an area of secret sin, we essentially allow the root of that thing to lie dormant in the soil of our lives only to produce something way more sinister at a later time.

> ❝ **WHATEVER YOU LEAVE UNADDRESSED IN YOUR LIFE WILL BE THE VERY DOORWAY FOR THE ENEMY.**

While the Gibeonites had a cleverly crafted tactic, it only worked because Joshua and the Israelites took things at face value. They examined the food but failed to consult the Lord. A poor evaluation, recognition or consideration of the wily way in which the enemy works will ultimately fool the ignorant believer. The truth is that while the enemy cannot rule you, he'll certainly try to fool you.

The enemy always works with façades and with a faux or counterfeit reality. As the king of lies, he cannot posses or dispense truth. However, he will play off truth to lure us into deception, since what is counterfeit can be difficult to discern.

If I learned anything in my short stint in retail it was how to identify fake or counterfeit currency. The managers would teach us to take the bill and hold it up to the light. It was then that you could see the genuine markings. This is the same way we are meant to see the enemy's counterfeit schemes. We need to hold them up to the light and weigh them against the Word of God.

If we were to read on in scripture, we would see that the Israelites were forced into battles that were not even theirs because of Joshua's poor assessment and this deceptive alliance. God had to rescue them from these battles.

Now before we go too hard on Joshua, we could easily be just as guilty of missing the devil's deception and traps in life. It can seem to be an obvious assault on our faith when we face strong opposition or when we're under attack in the classic areas like sickness, job loss or economic instability. But this is not the main way in which the enemy actually works. In fact, most of the time I don't even like giving the enemy the credit when it comes to these areas in life because I don't want to award him undue power in my world. I do know the way in which he most commonly works is through things like gossip, unforgiveness, pride and offense. The devil's aim with this is to corner us and ultimately divide us. All it takes is a seed of doubt.

That is exactly why, at Jericho and Ai, God instructed the Israelites to not leave anyone alive. At first read this sounds incredibly brutal and unnecessary, but God knew that any area the enemy is allowed to occupy will be the very root of division.

Paul feared this would take place within the church. The false apostles were literally dividing the church, and he understood fully that a house divided cannot stand. As a matter of fact, anything divided cannot stand: not a church, not a team, not a marriage. Paul makes his concern known to the church by expressing his fear that somehow their pure and undivided devotion to Christ will be corrupted. In our lives, much like the Corinthian church, a divided devotion is the fruit. The root, however, is always misplaced faith.

Allow me to explain.

Joshua, as the leader of the nation, was not only required to consult the Lord for guidance, but he was also instructed to consult the Lord for confidence. That would essentially set them up with the assurance that God was with them no matter what situation they would face. And this is God's way of loosening fear's grip in our life. We are pretty much guaranteed to face circumstances and situations that will intimidate us in this life. It is in those times—when we're under pressure and when the circumstances are beyond us—when God provides a pathway to His strength.

Yet, instead of putting stock in God's ability to navigate us through each season, we constantly assess our inability and often blurt out the sentence "I can't do this!"

It's subtle but exactly what Paul considers to be "misplaced faith."

The doctrine that Paul was confronting from the false apostles was one of self-promotion and glorifying one's ability apart from God.

And he says this: "But I don't consider myself inferior in any way to these 'super apostles' who teach such things. I may be unskilled as a speaker, but I'm not lacking in knowledge" (2 Corinthians 11:5-6, NLT).

In other words, Paul is saying, "I'm not stupid," or better still, "I ain't no fool." He was fully aware that without God he would still be stuck in his sin. The doctrine Paul preached was not one of man coming to God, but of God coming to man. So that statement, "I can't do this," is a matter of misplaced faith, because our faith was never meant to be in ourselves. It has always been designed to be in God.

Faith is a gift, a free gift that is given by God. And maybe you are reading this book and wondering why you did not get your full portion. But what is important to know is that faith is only ever given in seed form. There is something important that we have to do with it.

Let's find out together.

day twelve

DEBUNKING DECEPTION

"While the enemy cannot rule you, he'll certainly try to fool you."

Deception is defined as the act of deceiving someone by concealing or misrepresenting the truth. In our Christian walk, the devil's goal is to deceive you in this same way in order to put your calling into question.

We are meant to discover the enemy's counterfeit schemes by holding them up to the light and weighing them against the Word of God.

What scriptures illuminate the truth of God's Word over the enemy's lies in your life today?

_____

_____

_____

_____

_____

Despite our best efforts, there have likely been instances where we have fallen into the trap of the enemy and failed to consult God's truth. Thankfully, it is always within our power to change our perspective by bringing those areas to God.

In what ways has the enemy fooled you into a certain way of thinking but by faith you can reframe your perspective today?

_____

_____

_____

_____

_____

_____

_____

_____

_____

_____

_____

day thirteen

FAITH IN THE RIGHT PLACE

"When we're under pressure and when the circumstances are beyond us, God provides a pathway to His strength."

If I were to ask you who you had more faith in—yourself or God—I'm sure that you would answer "God." But I wonder if your actions truly reflect that belief. It is one thing to say that you trust in a big God; it is a whole other thing to act like you know that God is big, and you have faith in His ability to provide you with strength.

Reflect on the words you say and the actions you take. Who are you putting your faith in today—yourself or God?

_____

_____

_____

_____

_____

_____

_____

_____

_____

_____

_____

_____

_____

_____

_____

_____

The Hebrew word for the glory of God is kavod, which literally translates to "weight." When we give glory to God for His strength, His majesty, and His faithfulness, we are transferring the weight of our lives onto Him.

In what ways can you put more weight on God's ability to navigate you through each season?

_____

_____

_____

_____

_____

_____

_____

_____

_____

_____

_____

_____

6

THE GIFT OF FAITH

Adoni-zedek, king of Jerusalem, heard that Joshua had
captured and completely destroyed Ai and killed its king, just
as he had destroyed the town of Jericho and killed its king.
He also learned that the Gibeonites had made peace with
Israel
and were now their allies.
He and his people became very afraid when they heard all
this
because Gibeon was a large town—as large as the royal
cities and larger than Ai.
And the Gibeonite men were strong warriors.
So King Adoni-zedek of Jerusalem sent messengers to several
other kings:
"Come and help me destroy Gibeon," he urged them,
"for they have made peace with Joshua and the people of
Israel."
So these five Amorite kings combined their armies for a
united attack.
They moved all their troops into place and attacked Gibeon.
The men of Gibeon quickly sent messengers to Joshua at his
camp in Gilgal. "Don't abandon your servants now!" they
pleaded.
"Come at once! Save us! Help us! For all the Amorite kings
who live in the hill country
have joined forces to attack us."

JOSHUA 10:1-6 (NLT)

As a dad, I have realized that I think practically; whereas, as a mom, Keira thinks protectively. The other day, Keira and I were chatting with one of the VIVE Youth team as we were trying to strategize a way to make a youth event more accessible to more young people. During the conversation, I was getting creative and suggested they could catch the train. Now, I work under the premise that in a creative meeting there are no bad ideas. However, this idea was apparently really bad.

Madiha, my eldest daughter, who attends our youth ministry, overheard our conversation and said, "You would let me catch the train at night?"

Keira replied, "Oh, honey. I'm so sorry, but you don't have the street smarts to be on a train at night!"—alluding to the fact that, not only had I suggested a stupid idea, but our daughter was also pretty sheltered.

To which Madiha responded, "Mom, I have the street smarts to *not* get on a train at night!"

Now, you would think that over time I would learn some things. For example, Keira and I have been married for 16 years. Yet, do you know what I now know about women from being a husband and a father of daughters?

Absolutely nothing!

In all seriousness, this book has been designed to grow your faith in such a way that you would actually know what is possible in this life—or even better, that you would grasp not just the possibility of faith but the probability of faith and to be fully persuaded that with God all things are possible. Despite any circumstantial problem or situational roadblock, God's plan can and will prevail through the tangible medium of faith.

So far we have witnessed the power of God on display as the Israelites have stepped into the Promised Land, which, incidentally, was also enemy territory. We have been connecting their story with situations and circumstances in our own lives that similarly hold fear and uncertainty. What's been fascinating to explore is just how much of their uncertainty and the fear we face in this life actually come from the unknown.

The Bible reveals a clear connection between faith and the unseen. Faith is firmly found beyond what we can at times visualize or even recognize. In saying that, though, I want to make sure I am not confusing anyone by somehow inferring that we are simply meant to have a blind faith. That's not what I am implying at all. In fact, what I'm talking about is not a blind faith but a *bold* faith!

Blind faith is rooted in ignorance and is unaware of what's at stake. Bold faith counts the cost, is aware of adversity, but still decides to step.

Bold faith is the kind of faith that Hebrews talks about: "Now faith is being sure of what we hope for and certain of what we do not see" (Hebrews 11:1, NIV).

In other words, faith is having a confidence beyond what we can see and understanding that hope is a firm anchor to hold on to.

"BLIND FAITH IS ROOTED IN IGNORANCE AND UNAWARE OF WHAT'S AT STAKE. BOLD FAITH COUNTS THE COST, IS AWARE OF ADVERSITY, BUT STILL DECIDES TO STEP.

Still, how do we have a bold faith that does not ignore the realities of the circumstances? If blind faith is not being aware of what's around us, then what is bold faith? Or maybe worded more spiritually, how do we see the unseen?

I'm sure Joshua could help us some more.

As we discovered in an earlier chapter, Joshua was previously deceived by the Gibeonites. They pretended to be from a foreign land in order to establish a treaty with the Israelites. Joshua made the mistake of examining their food but not consulting the Lord—a foolish mistake that was drawing them into a battle that was not theirs, a battle that, because of the treaty, required them to engage in their newly formed ally's fight.

In every other battle up to this point, the Israelites faced them in obedience to the command of God. Working in obedience to the call of God brings some comfort to know that if God is the one who is sending us, then He will make a way to protect us. After all, every good Christian soldier knows that the "battle is not yours; the battle is the Lord's"—right?

But what about when the battle is yours? I'm talking about those fights that you find yourself in and the trouble that you get yourself into. That debt, that divorce, even that dumb decision that no one made but you. Is God going to get you out of messes that you get yourself into?

In this particular story, we have Joshua in such a mess. We find him in an awkward position as a result of his own poor decision.

Sometimes the miracle we are believing for is simply to get ourselves out of the mess that was our own doing. Those are the situations in life when the enemy comes at us through the regret of our past mistakes.

If you have figured out anything about the enemy at this point, then you have probably realized that his aim is to disqualify you by undermining your confidence. He wants to intimidate you with regret so that he can trap you in the mistakes of the past. But what I want to show you is not only how the enemy tries to work in our life, but also how God wants to work even through your mistakes. Some of the greatest miracles you will experience in life can come out of your worst mistakes.

As we are about to see in this story of Joshua, even though he was the one who got himself into this mess, God was going to be the one to get him out of it. Upon entering the battle, God powerfully shows up, causing Joshua and his army to be victorious. In verse 12, we see one of the greatest miracles recorded in the Bible, which also happens to be the reason Joshua was victorious:

> On the day the Lord gave the Israelites victory over the Amorites, Joshua prayed to the Lord in

front of all the people of Israel. He said, "Let the sun stand still over Gibeon, and the moon over the valley of Aij-a-lon." So the sun stood still and the moon stayed in place until the nation of Israel had defeated its enemies.

(JOSHUA 10:12-13, NLT)

Go ahead and bookmark this for a minute, because I want to parallel it with another story in the Bible.

In Mark 4, we see a well-known story where Jesus is asleep in a boat during a storm. In this New Testament story, we see that the disciples awaken Jesus, frantically wondering if He cares that they are going to drown. Then, in an amazing display of power and authority, Jesus speaks and calms the very wind and waves. What this revealed was a firsthand example to the disciples of exactly what Jesus was capable of. When you really know what God is capable of, it certainly builds faith. In scripture we get a front-row seat to the miracles, the signs, and the wonders that Jesus performed—just like the disciples. Yet what's interesting is that when the waves die down and the wind stops, Jesus asks them two questions: "Why are you afraid? Do you still have no faith?" (Mark 4:40, NLT).

The Bible version you have probably places a chapter marker at this point. But what we see in Mark 5 is actually a continuation of the story, because it tells us that as the boat reaches the shore, they are met by a demon-possessed man:

This man lived among the burial caves and could no longer be restrained, even with a chain. Whenever he was put into chains and shackles—as he often was—he snapped the chains from his wrists and smashed the shackles. No one was strong enough to subdue him. Day and night he wandered among the burial caves and in the hills, howling and cutting himself with sharp stones. When Jesus was still some distance away, the man saw him, ran to meet him, and bowed low before him. With a shriek, he screamed, "Why are you interfering with me, Jesus, Son of the Most High God? In the name of God, I beg you, don't torture me!" For Jesus had already said to the spirit, "Come out of the man, you evil spirit." Then Jesus demanded, "What is your name?" And he replied, "My name is Legion, because there are many of us inside this man." Then the evil spirits begged him again and again not to send them to some distant place. There happened to be a large herd of pigs feeding on the hillside nearby. "Send us into those pigs," the spirits begged. "Let us enter them." So Jesus gave them permission. The evil spirits came out of the man and entered the pigs, and the entire herd of about 2,000 pigs plunged down the steep hillside into the lake and drowned in the water. The herdsmen fled to the nearby town and the surrounding countryside, spreading the news as they ran. People rushed out to see what had happened. A crowd soon gathered around Jesus, and they saw the man who had been possessed by the legion of demons. He was sitting there fully clothed and perfectly sane, and they were all afraid. Then those who had seen what happened told the others about the demon-possessed man and the pigs. And the crowd began pleading with Jesus to go away and leave them alone.

(MARK 5:3-17, NLT)

Again, we see a powerful display of the authority of Jesus. Just like with the winds and the waves, even evil spirits submit to Jesus' authority. But something about this story has confused me and frustrated me as a student of God's Word and is a question that maybe you've wondered also: why would Jesus be merciful to demons?

The Bible says that the demons begged Jesus not to send them away, but instead He sent them into a large group of pigs nearby. Surely Jesus knew that simply casting the demons out would have had the same result and possibly even been better.

I mean, had He not sent them into the pigs He would have

- Set the man free,
- Further amazed the disciples at His authority,
- Avoided angering the people because of the loss of the pigs, and
- Saved all of that bacon!

But maybe the pigs play a more important part in this story than first thought. This passage actually reveals very little about what the demons wanted. It does, however, have a lot to do with what the disciples needed. Jesus' intended purpose in this fascinating decision to send the legion of demons into the pigs was not just to display again the authority He possessed, as He had revealed that emphatically with the wind and the waves already. No, Jesus was showing them another vital component to building bold faith.

The way you respond to situations in life is a direct reflection of two things: first, what you believe about God's capability, and second, what you believe about His character.

Notice that it was the loss of their pigs that caused the villagers to reject Jesus—and somewhat rightly so, I mean this was their income stream and their livelihood. This was not a small amount of pigs; it was all 2,000 of them.

Out of pure curiosity and intrigue, I had my assistant do some research for me around the price of pigs in today's economy just so that we could have a clearer understanding of the villagers' loss. I had her call farms directly and even use online sales websites to get the best price on pigs. She discovered that potbellied pigs average about $2,000 per pig in our area.

But, I thought, *surely there are cheaper pigs.* She kept searching and found that another seller was selling the average domestic pig for $500 per pig. Still, that seemed expensive to me. The search continued until she came across what was the best deal she could find for one-off pigs sold online. Now to get 2,000 pigs that way would take a lot of searching, but each pig would come in at $380.

That means that at the lowest possible price in today's market, the replacement value of 2,000 pigs would be roughly $760,000—not only is that expensive, but so much higher was the value of one life to Jesus!

You see, the disciples needed to see not just the capability of Jesus but also the character of Jesus. We get yet another picture of the nature and character of Jesus in scripture through the parables of the lost sheep, the lost coin, and the lost son.

That Jesus would sacrifice everything for *one*—this is illogical economy, friends. Yet the value of a life is immeasurable to Jesus.

Coming back to Joshua 10, as I said, we have one of the most incredible miracles recorded in the Bible. But the focus and the emphasis of this passage are not on the miracle as much as on the prayer. As you read about how the sun stood still, what stands out is exactly how God responds to faith!

Consider the boldness of this prayer that Joshua makes in the midst of the battle. He is in front of the entire nation of Israel. It is a bold ask, and yet Joshua knew that God was able. Joshua knew that God was sovereign, and because it was a sovereign God who made this world, God is able to step into it at any time He wants and suspend the natural laws that He Himself put in place.

It is great to pray bold prayers knowing what God can do. But Joshua did not just pray from knowing God's capability. Joshua prayed this prayer because knowing His character and knowing His capability mean having an understanding of what He can do. Knowing God's character explains why He will do it.

Pray those kind of prayers—the sun-stand-still kind of prayers—over your own life, family, and finances—

because God gives us permission to do so in His Word. Hebrews makes this clear:

"So God has given both his promise and his oath. These two things are unchangeable because it is impossible for God to lie. Therefore, we who have fled to him for refuge can have great confidence as we hold to the hope that lies before us."

(HEBREWS 6:18, NLT)

What gives us confidence beyond knowing what God can do is knowing who He is. This has affected and influenced my faith on a whole new level. To know what I know should affect what I believe for.

My prayer is that as followers of Jesus, we would pray bold prayers of faith. We would pray from the understanding of not just what God can do but also why He will.

If we look again at the situation with the pigs, Mark records that "As Jesus was getting into the boat, the man who had been demon possessed begged to go with him. But Jesus said, 'No, go home to your family, and tell them everything the Lord has done for you and how merciful he has been'" (Mark 5:18-20, NLT).

Surely it would be better stated to tell about how powerful the Lord had been or how capable the Lord had been. But that was not Jesus' instruction. Instead, He said to tell of how merciful He had been, to tell of the very character and nature of His love.

When we realize the character of God along with the capability of God, these two elements provide a platform of faith that will have a great effect. This is how you have bold faith. This is the gift of faith.

day fourteen
BLIND FAITH VS BOLD FAITH

"Blind faith is rooted in ignorance and is unaware of what's at stake. Bold faith counts the cost, is aware of adversity, but still decides to step."

Have you ever done a trust exercise? Usually it involves someone falling straight backwards—eyes closed—into the arms of someone else, praying that they catch you before you hit the ground. I am so glad that putting faith in God is nothing like a trust exercise.

God does not ask us to trust blindly. He has given us example after example, in both the Bible and in our own lives, of His faithfulness. Not only that, but He has made it very clear that we will encounter trials in this life—especially if we choose to follow Jesus. He does not promise an easy road, but He does tell you that He will be "with you always, even to the end of the age" (Matthew 28:20, NLT).

As I said before, bold faith counts the cost, is aware of adversity, but still decides to step.

How can you take another step of faith in your situation today?

When we truly understand the character of God, we have increased boldness in our faith. Here are some names used in the Bible to refer to God that reveal aspects of His character:

- Yahweh – "I AM" (Exodus 3:13-14, NLT)
- Abba – "Father" (Galatians 4:6, NLT)
- El Roi – "The God Who Sees" (Genesis 16:13, NLT)
- El Shaddai – "God Almighty" (Genesis 17:1, NLT)
- Jehovah Rapha – "The Lord Who Heals" (Exodus 15:26, NLT)
- Yahweh Shalom – "The Lord is Peace" (Judges 6:24, NLT)

How can you be bolder as a result of understanding God's character and His ability?

_____

_____

_____

_____

_____

_____

_____

_____

_____

_____

_____

_____

_____

_____

_____

_____

_____

_____

_____

_____

_____

day fifteen

FAITH PRAYERS

"God is able to step into it at any time He wants and suspend the natural laws that He Himself put in place."

In Joshua 10, Joshua prays to God to ask for the sun to stand still over their battlefield. Miraculously, it does just that! We serve a God who is not only able to answer big prayers but is willing to come to our aid when we need Him. God gives you permission in His Word to pray the sun-stand-still kind of prayers over your own life.

What three areas of your life need that prayer focus today?

_____

_____

_____

_____

_____

_____

_____

_____

_____

_____

_____

_____

_____

_____

_____

_____

_____

_____

_____

_____

_____

Find a miracle in the Bible that personally speaks to you. Maybe the miraculous healing of the woman with the issue of blood moves you. Maybe it is the resurrection of Lazarus, Jesus's good friend.

What does God reveal about Himself through that miracle?

_____

_____

_____

_____

_____

_____

_____

_____

_____

_____

_____

_____

_____

_____

_____

_____

_____

_____

_____

_____

_____

_____

_____

_____

_____

I challenge you today to pray for that same type of miracle in your own life.

7

FLIMSY FAITH

Joshua conquered all these kings and their land in a single campaign, for the Lord, the God of Israel, was fighting for his people.

JOSHUA 10:42 (NLT)

Life, I have found, is simply a series of decisions. Some you navigate well and others you tend to regret. When interviewed one time in a short film for a youth festival, I was asked if I have any regrets in life. Most people probably have some really cool answer for that question, like "I have regrets but wouldn't make any changes" or something brilliant like that. But when I was asked, I had to be honest. To this day there is a decision I do regret making.

When I was in junior high, my brothers, my buddies and I were into rollerblading. And before you laugh out loud, I'm not referring to inline skating, or gliding around beach sidewalks in tight pants. I'm talking about ramps, stairs and the occasional full-contact roller hockey. In fact, we would spend most of our weekends rollerblading at the local schools, finding stairs to jump off. Now this one Saturday we were at our local high school when a rival rollerblade crew turned up. We immediately knew that a stair-jump competition was required to stamp our dominance and protect our territory. After engaging in a few silent glances and head nods, we did the usual three stairs, five stairs, and even seven stair jumps, alternating as we went. But still neither crew had proven to be the better rollerbladers. This meant that we were going to have to take it to another level: an eight stair jump. None of us had ever done that many stairs before, so we were kind of nervous, even though we would never have shown it. And because I was born into a Christian household and firmly believed in the biblical model of firstborn birthright, I allowed my older brother to go first.

At this particular high school, there was only one set of eight stairs, which happened to be in front of the administration office. It had a short run-up, which meant that to make the landing you had to get maximum speed as quickly as possible. My brother pushed off the doors to the administration office but failed to get the required speed needed to make the distance, and he ended up landing on the bottom step. Fortunately for him, he was short for his age and, as he hit the step, he naturally tucked up into a ball and simply rolled away from the potential disaster fairly unscathed.

Next it was their turn, and I watched as their lead guy attempted the jump. Unfortunately for him, while he made the distance, he didn't keep his balance and ended up sliding along the concrete—grazing an arm and a leg.

Then the baton fell to me. After watching two guys fail, the pressure was on. I decided to go big or go home and lined up above the stairs. Before I could talk myself out of it, I pumped my legs as hard as I could, doing my best to get the required speed. Upon reaching the end of the runway, I launched myself with all my might, and to my momentary delight got more than enough height to make the distance. However, what is common knowledge in rollerblading is that the only thing worse than not enough air time is too much airtime. It just so happened that I had launched so hard that I severely overshot the landing. In fact, I had so much airtime that my right rollerblade had time to tuck itself underneath my backside so that upon impact with the ground the rear wheel hit with forceful impact right on the bullseye—like a judge's gavel on a striking block. I instantly shot up off the ground like a rocket and, without looking around or sticking around to be crowned as king of the hood,

I raced home so that my mum could inspect the damage!

Do I have any regrets? I'll let you decide.

But it's these mistakes we make in life that cause us to be overly cautious when making decisions—big decisions that is. I'm not talking about what take-out to order or even what vacation spot to book for summer break. I'm talking about the kind of decisions that determine the course and direction we take in life. I think we can agree that life holds some pretty heavy decisions for us to navigate: whether it's college, a career, or who we should marry.

It is said that, on average, as an adult we make over 35,000 decisions every day. Of course, not every decision is evenly weighted; some decisions we make simply out of habit and way too easy, like eating carbs even though we made a new year's resolution not to. Other decisions, however, may pose a bit more pressure, like the outfit we're going to wear to that job interview.

Actually, someone told me recently that the very reason CEOs like Mark Zuckerberg always wear the same outfit is because it is one fewer decision they have to make each day. In my mind, though, I think it is much easier to make a decision on what outfit to wear for the day than deciding on the outfit I'm going to wear for the rest of my life!

This is when decision-making gets real, when it holds some kind of bearing on my future—when the decision that is before me has the ability to direct or affect the very course of my life. I mean, these are not just decisions you want to get right; they are certainly not decisions you want to get wrong. While it's exciting to think about marrying the right person, it's terrifying to think about the possibility of marrying the wrong one.

When it comes to the career path I should choose, should I focus less on career and more on calling? Or is my career connected to my calling?

Maybe I can take us even deeper into the tension we experience as followers of Jesus, because I think we would like to know how to make decisions in line with God's will and not just based on what we want. The fear attached to this notion is what ultimately keeps us stuck when trying to choose what is right in life.

Now, if you are reading this and you are the kind of person who has a difficult time knowing exactly what God has for you or what God wants you to do, then let me tell you, so do I.

Can I be real with you? You know what I find really annoying? I find it really annoying how clearly and easily some people seem to hear from God. Do you know anyone like this?

These are the people who are always super-confident in what God said. They are the kind of people who always have a very detailed description of what God told them. But what about those of us with more of a flimsy faith? How can we find the confidence to make bold decisions and then stay confident in the decisions we have made?

Maybe we could explore some different expressions of confidence, because surely confidence is key in a decision-making ability—right?

Scripture certainly suggests so. One biblical author by the name of James addresses the very idea of confidence in his letter. And in a somewhat confronting passage, he directs his attention to a specific group of people, saying, "Come now, you who say, 'Today or tomorrow we will go into such and such a town and spend a year there and trade and make a profit'—yet you do not know what tomorrow will bring. What is your life?" (James 4:13-14, ESV).

In other words, James carries a concerned tone while addressing those who are so seemingly self-confident in this life. James was not only an apostle, but he was also a pastor, which means he wrote into real-world problems. When reading James, we need to appreciate that he is going to look at faith from a human perspective; or, in other words, James is only interested in the kind of faith that will actually direct us in everyday decisions. More than anything else, James wants to produce a faith that works in the life of every believer. From his own admission, his main concern for the church was that somehow their faith might be built upon wishful thinking rather than the very Word of God.

Now, in a similar vein as Joshua and Paul, if we were to follow along with the journey of James, we may be just as surprised at the level of his confidence. In fact, I might be so bold to say that if James had a word to describe his own faith, he might have used the word "flimsy."

This is simply because, depending on where you are reading about James in the biblical narrative, you will find a vastly different person. James was the half-brother of Jesus, born to Mary and Joseph. At the time of writing the previous passage, we find James as an apostle leading the church in Jerusalem. But if we were to backtrack to the early stages of Jesus' ministry, then we would find a different James—a skeptical brother.

We see in chapter 7 of John that James and his other brothers are mentioned:

> After this, Jesus traveled around Galilee. He wanted to stay out of Judea, where the Jewish leaders were plotting his death. But soon it was time for the Jewish Festival of Shelters, and Jesus' brothers said to him, "Leave here and go to Judea, where your followers can see your miracles! You can't become famous if you hide like this! If you can do such wonderful things, show yourself to the world!" For even his brothers didn't believe in him. Jesus replied, "Now is not the right time for me to go, but you can go anytime."
>
> **(JOHN 7:1-6, NLT)**

Here we have James, along with the other half-brothers of Jesus, in complete disbelief. What would make for great preaching would be if scripture had recorded a life-altering moment where James was able to see firsthand a crazy miracle that Jesus performed and as a result had great faith.

Peter and the other disciples saw Jesus walking on water! What a life-altering moment it would have been if James had caught Jesus flying or something crazy. But the Bible does not say anything like that. Actually, you would be hard-pressed to find James mention much at all in scripture and certainly nothing connected to a life-altering miracle.

Rather, we see the same James who was skeptical now leading the church with a bold confidence in the birthplace of the Christian faith. What shifted with James that gave him such confidence?

James might not have gotten an audible from heaven, or an angelic message, or a miracle, or even a specifically recorded sign, but James learned how to work with a flimsy faith.

Let me pose this question: how do you measure faith?

The Bible tells us in Matthew 17:20 that if you have even a mustard seed-sized faith, then you can move mountains. This is a great illustration of the power of faith, but how do I know how much faith I have? On Sunday morning at church, man, I'm full of faith. Just show me a mountain on Sunday morning, because I'm ready to move it. But what about in the real world? What about that financial mountain known as debt? How do I have the faith to move that mountain? And is the same faith I have on Sunday the same amount that I have on Monday?

What if all the faith I have is flimsy and fragile?

I often meet up with all kinds of people at many of the different conferences and events I attend, including entrepreneurs and church planters. They will sometimes make a comment about the fact that we started five churches in our first five years, saying, "God must have spoken really clearly for you to make that decision."

I always find myself reluctantly replying, "Well, kind of?"

After seeing the perplexed look on their face, I will

often follow up with, "To be honest, at the time that God spoke, it wasn't even that clear."

It was the same way when God spoke to us about moving to California to start our first church. We only kind of had a small word from God, which in reality was kind of flimsy. Truth be told, people would often ask us, "Why San Francisco?"

Because I never had a convincing reason, I would simply say, "Why not?"

I am very well aware that this story scares people, because we want something concrete. We expect that the bigger the decision, the more God must speak. I have had countless people sit across my desk or over coffee outline extremely detailed plans that God gave them, or tell me word for word all that God had spoken to them. And I simply sit there in utter amazement knowing that I am a pastor, and God has never spoken to me in that much detail.

Most of the time I consider my faith flimsy at best, because more often than not I have very little to go off of. Even when it came to deciding that our fifth location would be in Rome, Italy, God gave us just two words: "What if?"

There were no signs. I did not stumble across an ancient artifact on a Roman street with the word "VIVE" inscribed on it. I simply had the impression *what if?*

What if faith is not measured in how detailed God speaks to you but is based on your obedience to one simple word? As scripture tells us, and as we have already highlighted in this book, faith is the substance of things hoped for and the evidence of things unseen.

When we look to define God's leading through a detailed articulation, we run the risk of substituting God's voice for our own internal dialogue. This is why we get stuck when making big decisions—because we try to look for confidence in ourselves.

> **WHEN WE LOOK TO DEFINE GOD'S LEADING THROUGH A DETAILED ARTICULATION, WE RUN THE RISK OF SUBSTITUTING GOD'S VOICE FOR OUR OWN INTERNAL DIALOGUE.**

James had a real issue with this. When James and his brothers were mocking Jesus, It is interesting what Jesus responded this way:

> "For even his brothers didn't believe in him. Jesus replied, 'Now is not the right time for me to go, but you can go anytime.'"
>
> **(JAMES 7:5, NLT)**

Self-confident faith is the kind of faith that requires God to move first. It is like being able to articulate every move before you even make one.

James discovered something about prayer.

We see that, through scripture, his prayer changed from a self-confident prayer to a Christ-confident prayer. In verse 15, James teaches us how to pray in such a way that we put our confidence in Christ:

"Instead you ought to say, 'If the Lord wills, we will live and do this or that.'"

(JAMES 4:15, NIV)

So much of our fear comes from wondering about God's will. I like what James instructs: "If the Lord wills, we will." What if instead of wanting God to move, God wants the same from us?

What do I mean?

We get stuck wondering if God is willing. Maybe we need to be asking, "Am I willing?"

Maybe all you have is flimsy faith. Maybe all you have is mustard-seed faith. But maybe it is far less about the mountain and way more about what a little, flimsy, fragile faith can do.

Joshua displayed this kind of faith 40 years before he was commissioned to lead God's people into the Promised Land. If you recall, Joshua as a young man was only one of two spies that reported on the Promised Land with a positive perspective. This was not because Joshua was so confident in his fighting skill or the ability of the Israelites; after all, they had been slaves their entire life without any military training. No, Joshua was confident because he had just had a firsthand experience of what God could do in bringing His people out of captivity. At best, Joshua had a flimsy faith. In the beginning, Joshua knew where his victory would come from. Later in Joshua's life, we see that after many battles, "Joshua conquered all these kings and their land in a single campaign, for the Lord, the God of Israel, was fighting for his people" (Joshua 10:42, NLT).

Joshua knew that it was God who would fight for him. So often we get stuck in fear based on our ability to navigate situations and circumstances of life. What if we were to have, like Joshua, the firm understanding that God's got us?

day sixteen

DECISION MAKING

"When we look to define God's leading through a detailed articulation, we run the risk of substituting God's voice for our own internal dialogue."

Making decisions—especially the most important decisions—can be scary. We worry that we will make the wrong choice, because we don't want to suffer consequences that can result from our own mistakes. If you are like me, you would rather make decisions in line with what God wills. Nevertheless, it can be hard to know what is God's will versus my own will.

How can you delineate between God's voice and your own voice?

_____

_____

_____

_____

_____

Decision making becomes way easier when you realize that it is less about the exact decision you make and more about the posture you take when making that decision. We should approach our decisions with the understanding that it is confidence in God and not confidence in ourselves that gives us faith that the outcome will be victorious.

How would you do each day differently if you understood that God's got you?

_____

_____

_____

_____

_____

_____

_____

_____

_____

_____

_____

_____

_____

_____

_____

_____

_____

_____

_____

_____

_____

_____

_____

_____

_____

_____

day seventeen
OBEDIENCE

"What if faith is not measured in how detailed God speaks to you but is based on your obedience to one simple word?"

The word "obey" is not very popular. We usually associate it with negative things, like being forced to obey a parent's rules we didn't agree with. As a result, words like obedience and submission in the Bible can cause us to have a knee-jerk adverse reaction.

However, God makes it clear in His Word that obedience is actually one of the most positive things we can do in this life. Obedience opens the door for blessing. So many times in the Bible we find conditional blessings that hinge on our willingness to submit our will to God's will.

In Exodus 23:20 (NLT), God says, "But *if* you are careful to obey him, following all my instructions, *then* I will be an enemy to your enemies, and I will oppose those who oppose you."

In Malachi 3:10 (NLT), it says, "'Bring all the tithes into the storehouse so there will be enough food in my Temple. *If* you do,' says the Lord of Heaven's Armies, 'I *will* open the windows of heaven for you. I *will* pour out a blessing so great you won't have enough room to take it in! Try it! Put me to the test!'"

These blessings are all attached to "if" statements. God's blessing on our lives is often determined by the actions we take. God has the capacity to bless us and is willing to do so. But maybe we need to truly evaluate if we are willing.

Identify a situation in life where you have wanted God to move. Could God want you to move in that situation? Are you willing to do what it takes for it to come to pass?

_____

_____

_____

_____

_____

_____

_____

_____

_____

_____

_____

8

HOW TO HAVE FAITH WHEN YOU DON'T HAVE CONTROL

*When King Jabin of Hazor heard what had happened,
he sent messages to the following kings: King Jobab of
Madon; the king of Shimron; the king of Acshaph;
all the kings of the northern hill country;
the kings in the Jordan Valley south of Galilee; the kings in
the Galilean foothills; the kings of Naphoth-dor on the west;
the kings of Canaan, both east and west; the kings of the
Amorites, the Hittites, the Perizzites,
the Jebusites in the hill country,
and the Hivites in the towns on the slopes of Mount Hermon
in the land of Mizpah. All these kings came out to fight.
Their combined armies formed a vast horde.
And with all their horses and chariots, they covered the
landscape like the sand on the seashore.
The kings joined forces and established their camp around
the water near Merom to fight against Israel.
Then the Lord said to Joshua, "Do not be afraid of them.
By this time tomorrow I will hand all of them over to Israel as
dead men.
Then you must cripple their horses and burn their chariots."*

JOSHUA 11:1-9 (NLT)

I really, really like being in control. But who doesn't? Nevertheless, what I have discovered as a leader, husband and dad is that rarely do I ever have it—control, that is.

Most of the time, life situations just come at us and it feels like we are simply reacting rather than being in control. For example, I can recall two major times when life felt way beyond my control.

The first time was at around 14 years old and involved hot summer winds, dry grass, brothers, and a single match. To save incriminating myself or my siblings, let's just say that a situation quickly got out of control, and although I'm glad to say that we stopped the wildfire from burning down the neighborhood, my eyebrows took some time to grow back.

The second time life suddenly presented me with the shocking revelation that I was not in control was when we went from one daughter to three daughters. You see, we skipped the two-daughter stage and jumped right into a family of five. I had only just acclimated to parent life and being a dad of a daughter when we discovered that Keira was pregnant again. Somewhat excited, but still nervous to add another baby to the mix, I went to the doctor's office for the first ultrasound of our family's new addition. While sitting next to Keira and watching the monitors as the doctor glided the scanner across her bulging belly, I noticed that the image was duplicated. At first I was confused, as I could clearly see two of the same baby, but I was convincing myself that it was some kind of special imaging the doctor must do to get a better reading. This was until he clinically delivered the news that this was a twin pregnancy.

At those words and all the sound became muffled, and as hard as I tried, I could not make out what anyone was saying. My mind was being bombarded with a million thoughts—mainly revolving around finances, the cost of having two babies, probably needing to get a second job, etc. I sat silently for the rest of the scan. At the end of our consult, the doctor asked me if I had any questions, and despite the fact that I had a billion, I simply stared at him and did not say a thing. I could not muster a word. I was shaken. Keira and I walked out into the parking lot and looked at each other. As we did, we both let out a sound at the same time. However, while hers was laughter and joy, I began to cry (happy tears, of course).

I was certainly excited for the adventure but felt ill equipped and well out of control. Actually, maybe we could commit a section of this book to discussing this concept.

Now, I say "concept" because the very idea of control is elusive at best. We love the notion of being in control, and that idea is certainly something that we would connect with confidence in life. By having control in a given situation, we believe that it should produce the certainty required to step out in faith. But what do you do when you realize that in life you have very little to no control?

When it comes to the circumstances we face and the unpredictable situations that life throws at us, we really do not have to live that long to realize that control is a fluid concept.

This revelation can cause paralysis in even the most gifted leader. Having to navigate the unknown while leading unpredictable people with a variety of personalities and individual preferences and proclivities can not only hinder a leader but may also be the very reason they give up and quit. This often stems from an understanding that we cannot control others' thoughts about us, their actions toward us, or their opinions of us. This knowledge is the very fuel that can feed anxiety, immobilize us, and be the cause for hesitation in our life.

We could spend a lot of time talking about what is out of our control, but we could just as easily talk about what controls us.

I'm talking about our emotions and expectations. I'm talking about comparison and condemnation. I'm talking about having elusive dreams that—no matter how hard you try or what you do—you cannot seem to make a reality.

Maybe it is wanting so badly to be a parent but being unable to produce the very thing you desire. And you know what is really confusing? When you know you are called but you are not in control.

I'm talking about when God gives you a task and something to build, but you just cannot seem to make it happen. This is often the case with church planters or business leaders who have heard clearly from God what to build. God has given us a picture, but for some reason we are stuck by circumstance or cornered by conditions that are out of our control. For Keira and me, we knew God was calling us to pioneer a move of God in major cities around the world, but the very idea of seeing revival in places like San Francisco and Rome seemed so far beyond our control.

So how do we pursue God's calling when we are clearly not in control?

If anyone could help us, I'm sure it's our man Joshua. As a Bible character, Joshua knew a little bit about being in situations beyond his control.

As we have established throughout this book, Joshua is the guy who was thrust into leading the Israelite nation after the death of Moses. He was not only unprepared and possibly ill equipped for the task (from a human perspective), but he was also now the one who was meant to be in control.

What defined the Israelites out of all the nations of the world as God's own people was what could only be described as the hand of God on the nation. As we see in scripture, God desired to carve out of all the nations of the world His very own possession, a people through which He could reveal His power, provision and protection. Time and time again we see God revealing His glory through incredible miracles that ultimately serve as a reminder to the Israelites that it is God who is in control.

This is a healthy understanding to have: while I don't have control, God does. In any given situation and no matter what mess I find myself in, God has a way out. I love this understanding and have leaned into it on many occasions in life. Just knowing that God has it means that even if you got yourself into a situation, God can get you out. In other words, God has your today, and He has your tomorrow. Even when you feel like you are out on the water and are sinking, God has you!

Under the new covenant, just like the Israelites, we are now also God's chosen people and His very own possession. The same hand of God that we see so evident in scripture is the same favor, anointing and power that now flows to us and through us: the very power of God to bring freedom and to be free. It is the yoke-shaking, bondage-breaking anointing from God. In fact, I think it would be crazy to think about what it would look like if the people of God actually understood what they have been empowered with. You see, the hand of God describes the supernatural power and anointing of God that is coupled with the purpose of God.

Another way to say it is that God anoints what He assigns.

We see this clearly in scripture with Jesus. The Gospel of Luke tells us that at the beginning of Jesus' ministry, as He came out of the wilderness after 40 days without food, Jesus stepped into the synagogue, opened the scroll of Isaiah to a particular place, and read aloud:

> The Spirit of the Lord is upon me, for he has anointed me to bring Good News to the poor. He has sent me to proclaim that captives will be released, that the blind will see, that the oppressed will be set free, and that the time of the Lord's favor has come.
>
> **(LUKE 4:18-19, NLT)**

Notice how Jesus made a clear definition and reason for His anointing. His anointing was for His assignment. Gifting is different from anointing. Giftings are given regardless of whether you use them. Paul tells us in Romans that God gives gifts and, under no circumstance, does He take them back. He says, " ... for God's gifts and his call are irrevocable" (Romans 11:29, NIV).

However, anointing is only activated upon assignment. If you want God's anointing, it's a really good idea to get on God's assignment.

This is what we see with Joshua and the Israelites. For generations the people had been living in captivity as slaves in Egypt. However, the moment Moses got on board with God's assignment, the power of God preceded him, and they were delivered by the mighty hand of God. Surely you have recognized the hand of God on your life at some point, in some way. Maybe that explains why you have the job that you do. Maybe it's the reason you are still breathing air. Maybe that explains how you have the wife that you do. If not for the hand of God. Christian maturity is the ability to recognize and acknowledge God's hand of blessing and glorify Him as a result.

However, recognizing the hand of God is one thing; activating and operating it (when you need it) can be frustrating.

Have you ever felt the frustration of needing direction in life and it seems like you cannot get God to speak? What would be nice would be if the hand of God could be like a magic wand and, given the situation, you could just wave it to work right when you wanted it to. Even though I understand and believe that God is in control and that my future is in His hands, I still wonder what part I play in the situation. Or in other words, if so much is in God's hands, then what is in my hands?

If I could summarize the story of Joshua, I feel this would be it: a man who experiences some of the most impressive displays of God's power in the whole Bible. I'm talking about the wall of Jericho, the sun standing still, the time when Joshua was fighting an enemy and God caused a severe hail storm to break out, which killed more of Joshua's enemies than the entire Israelite army could.

Yet, despite the evident mighty hand of God, we see a fascinating journey of Joshua discovering the part that he plays in the narrative.

In the story of Joshua, we witness the Israelites fighting battle after battle; but every place Joshua led the people to, the destination was not in his control. Instead of seeing a land flowing with milk and honey, they were experiencing opposition and enemies.

I have been to Israel. If I'm being honest, I questioned many times what was so good about that land. I know historically the land has been fought over, is highly sought after, and was the promise of God, but to me there is nothing appealing about it. The supposed Promised Land is dry, arid, rocky and barren. To me, it presents as a Promised Land that does not look so promising. I mean, why didn't God design the Middle East to be more like Hawaii or the Bahamas? As I read through the story of Joshua, I feel sorry for him. Here he is leading God's people along a path and to a place that is not in his control.

Have you ever found yourself stuck in a place that was not by your design?

Our Rome campus startup team members have

all moved from different parts of Italy. Some came from the north, an area known for its beauty and scenery. I found out during one of our conversations that moving to Rome was a stark contrast for them. The city of Rome is really old, which to tourists is the coolest thing ever. You have buildings still standing that are dated in the BC era. In fact, I have stayed in houses there that are older than the United States of America! It's cool to visit, but when you have to live there it's very different. I mean, the roads have potholes the size of small cars.

Now, what has been confronting to many of the team and is often the case for us in different seasons of life is to be in in the place God has called us but not so sure if we even like it. Not only is it unfamiliar, but what makes it uncomfortable is when things feel so far out of our control.

This was the case for Joshua. He was bringing the people of God into the land God had for them. However, not only were they unsure if they actually wanted it, but from the moment they stepped foot in the land, they have been fighting for what God had told them was already theirs. All the way up to chapter 11 in Joshua, we see Israel defeat city after city. Now we find all the kings from the north aligning and gathering their armies to stop the Israelites. The Bible says that the enemies were more numerous than the sand on the seashore. In other words, Joshua is in a situation beyond his control.

To make matters worse, God gives Joshua a bizarre command:

"Then the Lord said to Joshua, 'Do not be afraid of them. By this time tomorrow I will hand all of them

over to Israel as dead men. Then you must cripple
their horses and burn their chariots.'"

(JOSHUA 11:6, NLT)

This had to be so confusing. If I'm Joshua, I'm
thinking that not only is the Promised Land not so
promising, but now they cannot even keep the spoils
of war? These horses were not any ordinary farm
horses; they were battled-trained horses, something
that takes years to condition so that they do not
spook in the heat of battle. And the chariots had
been battle hardened. All these items would have
given the Israelites a major military advantage. Yet
God says to cripple them and burn them.

As I read this passage, I found myself getting
frustrated. The passage doesn't even go on to tell
us why God wanted Joshua to do this. No rhyme or
reason is given.

In a way, when we started VIVE Church, we found
ourselves in a similar situation. We had sown all our
finances into the church; and when I say "our"
finances, I literally mean our personal finances.

We did not have big churches supporting us;
instead, we had to sell everything we owned. My
daughters sold off their favorite toys, and we sold
possessions that held incredible sentimental value.
Nonetheless, we were confident that God had
everything in control. However, when we got here
and started building the church, the finances ran out
pretty quickly. We had just enough money for the
church and barely enough money for our family. At
one point we did not have enough money for health
insurance, so when Zali got pneumonia and had to

have an X-ray, we received an unexpected bill that was three times the price of my first car!

Despite the circumstances, we kept believing that God had it under control.

Then a few years into church planting, a well-known news media outlet approached us for an interview. Unbeknownst to us, they were trying to push the angle that we had started the church because there was so much money in this region. We naively thought they were genuinely interested in reporting on a rapidly growing church. Instead, we discovered that not only could we not control the situation we were in, but we also could not control what people made up about us.

I almost feel like Joshua is in a similar yet more severe situation. Not only can he not control the circumstances, but there also seems to be no reward for all his efforts.

Why would God ask Joshua to cripple the horses and burn the chariots? This passage confused me and confronted me for the longest time. At least you would think that the scripture would give you an immediate explanation or reason to the obscure order, but it does not. Actually, nowhere in the entire book of Joshua will you find an explanation for God's bizarre command.

However, in the midst of my frustration, God showed me something in Psalm 20. There are two verses that in my opinion should have been in Joshua, but for some reason God put them in the book of Psalms:

"Now I know that the Lord saves his anointed; he answers him from his holy heaven with the saving power of his right hand. Some trust in chariots and some in horses, but we trust in the name of the Lord our God."

(PSALM 20:6-7, NIV)

In other words, and this is important to know, Joshua could have kept the horses and chariots. However, that decision would have lifted God's hand of protection off the Israelites. It is evident that Joshua is not the one in control, which is the conclusion that life will bring you to and is a really tough pill to swallow for all the control freaks.

You do not have, never have had, and never will have control. The very concept of having control in life is elusive and an illusion, meaning that control is something that you only ever think you have. If you have not realized that yet, then you have not yet faced the battle that will show you how no amount of organizing, planning or scheming can stop the unexpected elements, disappointments, broken hearts and betrayals that will take place. These will be the battles that will serve as the very reminder that you do not have control.

But while it's true that you don't have control, you do have a choice.

" YOU DON'T HAVE CONTROL, BUT YOU DO HAVE A CHOICE.

Let's explore the idea of choice for a minute. No matter the situation, there is always a choice, and the fact that you do not have control does not mean that you don't have a choice.

What if I was to tell you that where you are in life is a sum total your choices?

We do not like hearing that. It's easier to blame others for what was done to us or to emphasize the fact that we did not have control in situations that led us to where we are in life. But I'm here to tell you that you always have a choice.

Joy is a choice. Others cannot make you happy and things cannot make you happy, because joy is a choice that you make. Peace is also a choice. In his letter to the Colossians, Paul says to "Let the peace of Christ rule in your hearts" (Colossians 3:15, NIV).

God says to Joshua after he sees the enemy, "Don't be afraid," indicating that fear is also a choice. If that is the case, then the opposite is also true. Faith is also a choice. I'm talking about perspective—not just what we see but also the way we see it. You could be asking God to take you to a different city, but maybe God is asking you to see your city differently. You can choose natural means or you can choose supernatural provision. Your perspective is your choice.

At every juncture, Joshua did not have control, but he did have a choice. In Joshua 6, we see the battle at Jericho. Joshua had no control over the wall that was opposing him, but he made a choice to march by faith. In chapter 10, Joshua is in a battle, and daylight is running out. For victory, he needs something that is out of his control. But instead of complaining, he chooses to pray, and God miraculously causes the sun to stand still in the sky.

You may have no control over the fact that you did not have a dad, but that does not mean that you cannot make the choice to be a good one. You may have had no control over how someone mistreated you, but the choice is yours as to whether you are a victim or you walk in victory. You may have had no control over the fact that you were abused, but the power to forgive is your choice.

The devil does not have a choice; he's already defeated.

But both fear and faith are a choice. Faith is not about control; faith is not even about being certain, because, as Hebrews tells us, "Faith is the substance of things hoped for." I don't know, but I hope. I'm not sure, but I hope.

Actually, faith is a choice that, when made, moves the hand of God. What do I mean by that?

Just as Joshua could have chosen a natural means of warfare, so too you could put all your trust in your paycheck. This is why God gives us the principle of the tithe—so that we can either trust in ourselves or trust our finances to God.

Even when you have a situation beyond your control, you still have a choice. It took Joshua a lifetime of battles to learn this. At the beginning of the book of Joshua, we see Joshua as a young and bold leader, but by the end of the book, we find Joshua as an old man talking to the people of Israel.

It's in the final chapter of Joshua, in chapter 24, where we find Joshua's conclusion to a lifetime of battles:

And you went over the Jordan and came to Jericho, and the leaders of Jericho fought against you, and also the Amorites, the Perizzites, the Canaanites, the Hittites, the Girgashites, the Hivites, and the Jebusites. And I gave them into your hand. And I sent the hornet before you, which drove them out before you, the two kings of the Amorites; it was not by your sword or by your bow. I gave you a land on which you had not labored and cities that you had not built, and you dwell in them. You eat the fruit of vineyards and olive orchards that you did not plant. Now therefore fear the Lord and serve him in sincerity and in faithfulness. Put away the gods that your fathers served beyond the River and in Egypt, and serve the Lord. And if it is evil in your eyes to serve the Lord, choose this day whom you will serve, whether the gods your fathers served in the region beyond the River, or the gods of the Amorites in whose land you dwell. But as for me and my house, we will serve the Lord.

(JOSHUA 24:11-15, ESV)

Maybe you could consider what situation or condition you are facing that is beyond your control. What choice is God presenting you with today?

day eighteen

CENTRAL PROCESSING UNIT

"Have you ever found yourself stuck in a place that was not by your design?"

All computers have a CPU (Central Processing Unit). As humans, we do too; it's called our mind. So much of our outlook is determined by the way that we process the information we receive.

In most cases, we don't control the information that we receive. More often than not it probably feels like life is happening to us, and it is completely out of our control. We are left to decide what to do with what we are given.

If we cannot change what we receive, how can we change the way we process?

_____

_____

_____

_____

_____

The CPU of a computer exists to employ the instructions of the computer's programs. It receives an input and provides an output that is based on the systems in place. In similar fashion, we usually have habits of response to the negative situations we experience in life. It is one thing to talk about changing the way we process information, but we need to have personal habits that help us to do that well.

What systems or habits can you put in place in your life to help you change the way you process the circumstances of life?

_____

_____

_____

_____

_____

_____

_____

_____

_____

_____

day nineteen
YOU STILL HAVE A CHOICE

"God has your today, and He has your tomorrow."

God exists outside of time in the way that we know it. The Bible actually refers to two different types of time: chronos and kairos. The ancient Greek word chronos refers to the chronological time we live in. It counts down by days and minutes, and there never seems to be enough of it. Kairos time speaks of a divine and opportune time where God intercepts chronos time to cause something to occur.

This understanding of time is great news for us! It means that no matter what we are going through, God has it under control and can move in a moment to change everything. We cannot control much in this life, and we certainly cannot control time. But you can rest assured that the God who moves outside of time has got you—no matter what!

In what ways has God shown you that He is in control?

Even in situations beyond your control, you still have a choice. You do not have to simply be a victim of your circumstances. Joshua entered many battles where he was out of control, but he chose to have faith in God and watched many miraculous victories come about as a result.

What things are currently out of your control, and what choices can you make?

_____

_____

_____

_____

_____

_____

_____

_____

_____

_____

_____

_____

_____

_____

_____

_____

_____

_____

_____

_____

_____

_____

_____

_____

_____

_____

_____

9

THE FIGHT OF FAITH

A delegation from the tribe of Judah, led by Caleb son of
Jephunneh the Kenizzite, came to Joshua at Gilgal. Caleb
said to Joshua, "Remember what the Lord said to Moses, the
man of God,
about you and me when we were at Kadesh-barnea.
I was forty years old when Moses, the servant of the Lord,
sent me from Kadesh-barnea to explore the land of Canaan.
I returned and gave an honest report, but my brothers who
went with me frightened the people from entering the
Promised Land.
For my part, I wholeheartedly followed the Lord my God.
So that day Moses solemnly promised me,
'The land of Canaan on which you were just walking will be
your grant of land and that of your descendants forever,
because you wholeheartedly followed the Lord my God.'
"Now, as you can see, the Lord has kept me alive and well
as he promised for all these forty-five years since
Moses made this promise—even while Israel wandered in the
wilderness.
Today I am eighty-five years old. I am as strong now as I was
when Moses sent me on that journey, and I can still travel
and fight as well as I could then.
So give me the hill country that the Lord promised me.
You will remember that as scouts we found the descendants
of Anak living there in great, walled towns. But if the Lord is
with me,
I will drive them out of the land, just as the Lord said."

JOSHUA 14:6-12 (NLT)

There are two types of people in this world: there are lovers, and then there are fighters.

For much of my life, I certainly considered myself a fighter. I have three brothers, which meant that in our house I had to fight to survive. With Mum being the only female, it was certainly an atmosphere dominated by testosterone and violence. This meant growing up was not only a daily fight for food or the front seat of the car, but it was also a fight to simply prove our manhood. Naturally, when Keira and I got married, I considered my developmental years as training to protect her and look after her as a husband.

At Christmas time during our first year of marriage, there was a Carols by Candlelight event being held at a park near where we lived. It was a balmy December evening (as Christmas in Australia is during our summer season), and because of the heat there was plenty of, let's just say, "eggnog" being consumed. So much so that as we were leaving the park along with thousands of others at the end of the night, I noticed a guy up ahead of me causing some trouble. He thought it was hilarious to fall back on people behind him as the crowd congested together. He had certainly consumed too much and was finding so much joy in being a public nuisance. Seeing this take place, and now being a married man, I took it upon myself to act on behalf of my wife and the public to pull him into line.

I squeezed through the crowd and positioned myself right behind him. Watching him, I had noticed that right before he threw himself back on people, he would glance back to make sure someone was there and then launch himself into them, knocking them to the ground. As I was behind him, I saw him glance back. Sure enough he immediately proceeded to launch back at me. Since I was anticipating it, I simultaneously grabbed him by the collar and then forcefully assisted him to the ground with a heavy thud. I'm not sure if it was the adrenaline of the moment flowing through my veins or a sudden rush of blood to the head, but what came out of my mouth next was not planned. It just happened. Without thinking, I stood over him and yelled, "BOOM-SHAKA-LAKA!"

I mean, who says that?

As I was saying it I even wondered what I was saying and kind of trailed off—wanting to stop it from coming out. If that is not embarrassing enough, in my effort to impress Keira, I had failed to realize that this guy was not alone. He had a whole group of guys with him who had also been drinking a lot of "eggnog." They immediately turned around right at the moment I was standing over their friend shouting "BOOM-SHAKA-LAKA!"

They proceeded to get right up in my face and began pushing me back, saying way more colorful things than I had come up with. It took no time for me to regret my actions and realize that I was about to die. I was severely outnumbered and was preparing myself for a beating. In my mind I was thinking about how I could take one punch and then hit the ground and pretend to twitch, because no one wants to hit a twitching guy. To me that was the easiest and fastest way out of this situation. But right at that moment, as I was being shoved and was preparing to take a punch, out of nowhere came my hero. Keira jumped in front of me and started shoving the guys who were shoving me. She began to yell at them about just how frustrated everyone was of them and encouraging them to "back off."

To my surprise, they started to back away, saying, "Settle down, lady! We're just having fun."

The crowd at this point had circled around us and had started to applaud her. She then looked back at me and gave me a look as if to say, "Don't worry, I've got you."

The most confronting thing I realized in that moment was the revelation that in our relationship, I was actually the lover and she was the fighter!

As followers of Jesus, though, not only are we meant to be lovers, as most would expect, but like my wife, we have the capacity to be fighters too.

Let me show you how.

The apostle Paul had a consistent theme when writing to the different churches that he either began or felt led by the Spirit to shape. For example, to the Corinthian church, he begins his letter by informing them that they "have every spiritual gift you need as you eagerly wait for the return of our Lord Jesus Christ" (1 Corinthians 1:7, NLT).

In a similar fashion, Paul opens up his letter to the Ephesians by informing them that they also have been gifted in every possible way. He says, "All praise to God, the Father of our Lord Jesus Christ, who has blessed us with every spiritual blessing in the heavenly realms because we are united with Christ" (Ephesians 1:3, NLT).

This revelation is so powerful for us to grasp as the church: much of our spiritual breakthrough is held up in simple application of what is already ours. God has not held back anything from us but has released all authority, power and provision to us through our union with Jesus. You are not lacking in any way but are amply supplied with everything you need for the task that God has set before you. The apostle earnestly desired that we as the church would know exactly what we have in Christ as His children and heirs—that we would somehow wrap our minds around the incomparable strength available to us and our capacity to possess supernatural power as a flow on from knowing who we are in Christ.

He says, "And now you Gentiles have also heard the truth, the Good News that God saves you. And when you believed in Christ, he identified you as his own by giving you the Holy Spirit, whom he promised long ago" (Ephesians 1:13, NLT).

This is actually one of the greatest weapons of spiritual warfare: your identity in Christ. Knowing that you are no longer your own but that you have been bought with a price, and because through Christ you also overcame death, gives you more than mere confidence; it gives you a conqueror mentality. Did you know that spiritual warfare is not just for the elders of the church to stomp around in a prayer meeting? In reality, it is less about shouting down strongholds and way more about knowing who you are in Christ.

Actually, the spiritual battlefield is framed a little differently than most other forms of combat. Spiritual warfare is fought somewhat in reverse. In other words, it is kind of backward or even upside down. In most forms of combat, it is the strong who prevail; but in this war, it is when we are weak that we are strong. In most battles, we fight to be victorious; in spiritual warfare, we fight because we are already victorious.

Allow me to explain it like this: when you come into a relationship with Jesus, your life should look different as a result. That is because you now have a new normal that was not normal before Christ was in your life. For example, as a believer, it is normal to give your money away. As a follower of Jesus, it is normal to forgive people who wrong you. Your life is different from when you did not know Christ.

Before you knew Christ, first was first. But as a follower of Jesus, you discover that last is first. Before Christ, to get was to gain, but now to lose is to gain. No longer do you give and it is gone; now when you give, you receive. Romans 12 tells us that we overcome evil with good. James tells us that mercy triumphs over judgment. This is the new way to fight now that we have the Spirit of God at work within us. Paul says it like this:

> "Since this new way gives us such confidence, we can be very bold."
> **(2 CORINTHIANS 3:12, NLT)**

This kind of confidence, coupled with the understanding that we have everything we need to fulfill what God has called us to do, makes the believer dangerous to the enemy. It produces a boldness that, quite frankly, gives the devil nightmares. There is nothing more hazardous to the kingdom of darkness than a believer who is aware of their identity and authority in Christ Jesus. This is why the enemy so furiously attempts to intimidate us in the hope that we will forget everything we know and believe. This is also the very reason why the enemy does not want us discovering our gifts, calling, and anointing, because it is the very thing that makes us unstoppable for the kingdom of God.

Now, spiritual gifts have to be one of the coolest things in the kingdom of God. To know that God gifts us with unique abilities is crazy. We cannot do anything for them or to earn them; it's all God in His goodness deciding through His Holy Spirit that He wants us to have them. It's vital for us to understand that not only does the Holy Spirit give us gifts, but the Holy Spirit Himself is also a gift. In fact, there is an aspect of the Holy Spirit that I feel is often unidentified in the life of the believer: a tool that most are unaware of or, at best, struggle to utilize. But Paul reveals it to the Ephesians. He says, "The Spirit is God's guarantee that he will give us the inheritance he promised and that he has purchased us to be his own people. He did this so we would praise and glorify him" (Ephesians 1:14, NLT).

Have you ever heard the saying "There are no guarantees in life?" Or maybe you have heard this one: "The only certainty is death and taxes." Well, I want to argue those points, because the Word of God clearly contradicts those two statements. It hands us a tool that, when implemented, produces an unparalleled confidence. I mean, to have a personal guarantee from a friend is one thing, but when the guarantee comes from God Himself, that's a game changer. Paul reveals that the Spirit of God is our personal guarantee of God's promise—a guarantee that, despite any opposition we find ourselves facing, God's promise will prevail.

Now, I'm sure we can all recall situations and circumstances that were in clear opposition to God's calling. Maybe as you have been reading this book you have been in one of those very circumstances. Maybe you are facing financial opposition. Maybe you are experiencing opposition in the area of relationships. Maybe it feels like the very forces of nature are opposing your every step. Opposition is real, and you cannot have spiritual warfare without identifying the opponent. However, what can be disorienting is having a guarantee of complete victory but, because of opposition, you are seriously considering surrender.

How do we put God's guarantee to work in our life? How do we process the reality of opposition in situations beyond our control?

Well, something I have discovered is that God will often lead us into situations beyond our control as an opportunity to show us by His Spirit that He is the one in control!

Let me prove this to you with Joshua and the Israelites one more time. As we draw to the end of the Israelite journey, it could be helpful to go back to the beginning for a moment. Because while we have spent a lot of time with Joshua, there is another, less-identifiable character who may just minister to us.

If we were to go all the way back to where the entire nation of Israel was sitting on the outskirts of the Promised Land anticipating what God had for them, we would see that Moses commissioned twelve spies to enter it and bring back a report. Among those spies we know was Joshua. But Joshua had a counterpart by the name of Caleb. Caleb also walked the land and saw what God had promised through eyes of faith despite the evident opposition. This is recorded in the book of Numbers; so let's pick up the classic account right when the spies return from their mission:

> After exploring the land for forty days, the men returned to Moses, Aaron, and the whole community of Israel at Kadesh in the wilderness of Paran. They reported to the whole community what they had seen and showed them the fruit they had taken from the land. This was their report to Moses: "We entered the land you sent us to explore, and it is indeed a bountiful country—a land flowing with milk and honey. Here is the kind of fruit it produces. But the people living there are powerful, and their towns are large and fortified. We even saw giants there, the descendants of Anak! The Amalekites live in the Negev, and the Hittites, Jebusites, and Amorites live in the hill country. The Canaanites live along the coast of the Mediterranean Sea and along the Jordan Valley." But Caleb tried to quiet the people as they stood before Moses. "Let's go at once to take the land," he said. "We can certainly conquer it!" But the other men who had explored the land with him disagreed. "We can't go up against them! They are stronger than we are!" So they spread this bad report about the land among the Israelites: "The land we traveled through and explored will devour anyone who goes to live there. All the people we saw were huge.
>
> **(NUMBERS 13:25-32, NLT)**

Here we have an incredible illustration of exactly what we can so often see play out in our own lives. What God has for us is either blocked by our own negativity or is negated by the opinions of others.

I can clearly remember the process of revealing to people that we were going to move to the United States and start a church from scratch. At that time, we had not shared the news with many people because we were, quite frankly, still coming to terms with it ourselves. I would spend each morning at the running field prophesying into the future in an attempt to align my thoughts with God's Word. But as we began to tell people of our plans, they would often ask, "How do you know this is going to work?"— not "That's amazing" or "You guys have totally got this!" But everyone's responses were more along the lines of "Are you sure?"

Maybe I was too honest for my own good, but because I did not have a lot to come back to them with, I would simply tell them, "I don't know if it's going to work." I could see this confused them, because we appeared so confident. However, what can seem like confidence can actually be complete surrender.

There is so much power in surrender. When you surrender your thoughts and you surrender your fears, you find yourself beginning to believe that with God all things are actually possible. It's amazing what God can do with a life fully surrendered. I think we focus so much on getting what God has, but can God get what we have?

This is ultimately what it means to be filled with the Holy Spirit. Being filled with the Holy Spirit does not mean that God gives more of His Spirit; it simply means that I give the Holy Spirit more of me. That way I am truly being led by the Spirit of God through the avenue of surrender.

God has already given us every spiritual blessing. As a result, the questions are actually these: Have I given Him all of my heart? Have I given Him my finances? And what about my time and relationships? I really like the way John puts it. He says, "He must become greater and greater, and I must become less and less" (John 3:30, NLT).

In other words, being filled with the Spirit is not a one-time occurrence but a continual filling as we continue to surrender in greater measure. This is how the Holy Spirit gives us a continued confidence even in conflicting circumstance.

We see that Caleb and Joshua had a different report from the other ten spies. The other spies had a negative report, and because of their negativity, none of the people entered the Promised Land.

As a nation, they wandered through the wilderness for another forty years, and it's in the next chapter we see Moses appealing to God on behalf of the nation to not destroy the complaining people. It says this in verse 20 of chapter 14:

Then the Lord said: "I have pardoned, according to your word; but truly, as I live, all the earth shall be filled with the glory of the Lord—because all these men who have seen My glory and the signs which I did in Egypt and in the wilderness, and have put Me to the test now these ten times, and have not heeded My voice, they certainly shall not see the land of which I swore to their fathers, nor shall any of those who rejected Me see it. But my servant Caleb, because he has a different spirit in him and has followed me fully, I will bring into the land where he went, and his descendants shall inherit it.

(NUMBERS 14:20-24, NKJV)

Now, as I said earlier in this chapter, spiritual gifts are cool. Each of us possessing unique abilities and talents that differentiate us and align us with our individual calling is amazing. But when it comes to spiritual gifts, you may get stuck if you see those gifts as mere presents. Instead, what if you were to see spiritual gifts not only as presents but also as the presence of God? I say that because the Corinthian church was using spiritual gifts for self-elevation. They were treating the gifts of God as presents, like toys for enjoyment rather than tools for employment. God's plan for spiritual gifts is not only to reveal the job He has for you but also to equip you with tools for the task.

For ten of the twelve spies, the tool they forgot to employ was faith.

The enemy also has some tools of his own. By now we are all too familiar with his tool called fear. And we see this at work amongst the spies. But Caleb had a different spirit—a spirit of faith. What is interesting is that even though he had faith, he was still caught in circumstance. Caleb, along with the rest of the nation, still had to wander in the wilderness because of opposition. However, the Holy Spirit is our guarantee of God's presence despite circumstance.

This guarantee can keep us walking when we cannot see a way. Because Caleb had faith, he applied the tools God gave him—operating in the gifts of the Spirit—yet experienced opposition.

But something interesting is recorded in Joshua 14. It is here that we find the Israelites forty-five years later having entered into the Promised Land, and Joshua is dividing up the land to the descendants of Israel. Among the crowd is a once young and energetic leader, a man who faced his fair share of opposition, fought battles, and persevered. Caleb, who is still alive and now at the age of 85 years old, is ready to receive his reward.

We see that he came to Joshua to make his claim on what God had promised him:

A delegation from the tribe of Judah, led by Caleb son of Jephunneh the Kenizzite, came to Joshua at Gilgal. Caleb said to Joshua, "Remember what the Lord said to Moses, the man of God, about you and me when we were at Kadesh-barnea. I was forty years old when Moses, the servant of the Lord, sent me from Kadesh-barnea to explore the land of Canaan. I returned and gave an honest report, but my brothers who went with me frightened the people from entering the Promised Land. For my part, I wholeheartedly followed the Lord my God. So that day Moses solemnly promised me, 'The land of Canaan on which you were just walking will be your grant of land and that of your descendants forever, because you wholeheartedly followed the Lord my God.' Now, as you can see, the Lord has kept me alive and well as he promised for all these forty-five years since Moses made this promise—even while Israel wandered in the wilderness"

(JOSHUA 14:6-12, NLT)

To consider all the battles that we have talked about throughout this book, the opposition, the wandering and the waiting, and to realize that Caleb was there the entire time shows that it was not so much the presents of God that sustained him but the fact that His presence never left him. I'm sure there were some rough years. I'm certain that Caleb could recount some years when it did not look like he was going to make it, or some battles where he got wounded, or some season when he questioned God's timing; but if it had not been for the sustaining presence of the Lord that kept him alive, he would have missed out on his promise. If it had not been for His presence that continued to surround him even though circumstance contradicted what he had possibly pictured, he would not have made it.

I love what Caleb says next. This is possibly one of my favorite interactions in the entire Bible. He says, "Today I am eighty-five years old. I am as strong now as I was when Moses sent me on that journey, and I can still travel and fight as well as I could then. So give me the hill country that the Lord promised me" (Joshua 14:10-12, NLT).

I like the way the New King James version puts verse 12; it says, "So give me this Mountain..." (Joshua 14:12, NKJV).

You need to understand what Caleb is asking for, because the mountain he was referring to was still occupied by the enemy. The Israelites had defeated most of the occupying enemy but there were still strongholds that were yet to be conquered. The hill country was one of them. But Caleb was not settling for the comfortable second-place plains of the valley; he was holding on to a promise. I love what he goes on to say:

> "You will remember that as scouts we found the descendants of Anak living there in great, walled towns. But if the Lord is with me, I will drive them out of the land, just as the Lord said."
>
> **(JOSHUA 14:12, NLT)**

In other words, the very fact that the Lord is with us is our guarantee of complete victory—not our age, not favorable circumstance or the absence of opposition, not even our wisdom or experience. No, despite all of these things, and beyond God's "presents," it is God's unfailing presence that produces the faith to see what He promised come to pass. Sure, there may be giants that have held back the promise. There may have been circumstances beyond our control, but as long as the Lord is with us, victory is our guarantee.

> **"IT IS GOD'S UNFAILING PRESENCE THAT PRODUCES THE FAITH TO SEE WHAT HE PROMISED TO COME TO PASS.**

This should be your reminder that you are not done yet. You might be facing opposition, but know that greater is He who is in you than he who opposes you! One of the most powerful aspects of the Holy Spirit's work in your life is the simple truth that the Spirit is God's guarantee that what He said in His Word will come to pass.

What lies before you in any given situation is both fear and faith, opposition or opportunity. Life will present you with obvious intimidation. But God's plan is that, as you surrender to His purpose, walk in His presence, and discover His power, the fight of faith will be one you can easily win.

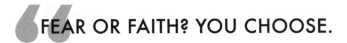**FEAR OR FAITH? YOU CHOOSE.**

day twenty
SURRENDER

"When you surrender your thoughts and you surrender your fears, you find yourself beginning to believe that with God all things are actually possible."

The kingdom of God works in a backwards economy. The Bible says that—in this kingdom—the first are last, and the last are first. It also says we fight *from* victory and not *for* victory. Maybe the most confusing is this: the more you give, the more you receive.

It can be confusing, because it is so contrary to what we are used to. Even the word "surrender" implies giving up a fight. Yet, in the kingdom of God, surrender is not about giving up the fight but truly getting in the fight. James 4:7 (NIV) says, "Submit yourselves, then, to God. Resist the devil, and he will flee from you." When you surrender your life to God, the Bible says that you are actually declaring war on the enemy. Surrendering to God isn't passive; it's an active declaration of victory for the kingdom of God over the kingdom of darkness. It is permitting the God of the universe to work for your victory on your behalf. There is so much power in surrender.

Have you given God all your heart, finances, time and relationships?

Sometimes people don't stay in the game long enough to see the promise fulfilled. The story of Caleb in the Bible is a striking example of the power of faith to birth incredible perseverance. After forty-five years of battles, Caleb was not just willing to continue the fight, but he was actively seeking to obtain God's promise on his life.

This kind of faith is only found within God's presence. The more you surrender of yourself, the more of Him you gain. The result: the drive and perseverance to fight the good fight of faith until the victorious end that God promises for all who believe in Him.

What disciplines or routines can you put into practice that will keep you connected to God's presence?

_____

_____

_____

_____

_____

_____

_____

_____

day twenty-one

YOU CHOOSE

"Fear or faith? You choose."

Fear and faith are both found in the realm of the unknown. But the effects of both on our lives don't have to be mysterious. I hope that through the journey of reading this book you have learned so much more about each one.

Outline the characteristics of both fear and faith that impacted you most below:

FEAR	FAITH

Identify a scripture about faith that you can hold onto when fear threatens to take hold:

_____

_____

_____

Knowing that both fear and faith are a choice, which will you choose today?

_____

_____

_____

_____

_____

_____

_____

_____

_____

_____

_____

_____

_____

BEHIND THE COVER

"Never judge a book by its cover" is certainly wise advice, because there is often more to the book than the cover can suggest. However, sometimes there is also more to the cover than first meets the eye.

This is certainly the case for *Faux Real*. You see, I wanted to communicate the central message of this book through the creativity of the cover itself and to put into picture what words can sometimes be difficult to explain—especially with a topic as elusive as fear and faith.

In staying in line with the theme of the book, on the cover is a brick wall with a section of rendering having fallen away with the brick being revealed. This pulls from the central theme of Joshua and the Israelites overcoming obstacles that were holding them back from their promise, especially the great walled city of Jericho. Jericho was a fortified city that stood between Joshua and the land God had called them to occupy. However, what the Israelites thought was behind the wall was not the reality. They expected a city full of warriors when what was really behind the wall was a people hiding and afraid for their lives. The cover art is meant to remind us that there is more to every circumstance than what is first perceived and that fear often has a way of presenting masks. When the outer covering falls away, like the great walls of Jericho did, what is exposed is often way less intimidating than first thought.

If you open the book, you will see that from cover to cover, it is one continuous image of a wall. But what you have most probably realized by now is that it is not actually a wall but a simple façade of a wall: a picture, mere wallpaper, a faux or fake wall, that appears real until you pull back the layer to show what is truly behind.

This is how fear works. It presents as intimidating and is very convincing until you see the crack, the chip or the hole that allows you a glimpse of what is really at work. While I see a wall, I'm locked out, but when I see that it's mere paper, I'm ready to burst through. My prayer is that this book will give you the run-up to burst through every fear façade that has held you out of God's promise.

NOTES

Chapter 1: Faux Fear

M. Night Shyamalan, director, *After Earth* (Sony Pictures Home Entertainment, 2013).

Chapter 2: Real Fear

Dr. Phil Pringle, *The Born Identity* (PaX Ministries Pty Ltd, 2015).

Chapter 3: The Fear We Need

"Ray Kroc Quotes," Quotes.net. STANDS4 LLC, 2018. Web. 23 Aug. 2018. <https://www.quotes.net/ quote/14932>.

ACKNOWLEDGMENTS

I can confidently say that I embarked on the journey of book writing somewhat naively, thinking it would be similar to preparing several sermons. I could not have been more wrong. This process has taught me a lot, and I am so thankful for those who have partnered and persevered with me along the way.

First, to my wife, Keira—Not only are you the source of much inspiration and illustration, but also you have truly taught me so much in the area of faith through your unwavering belief in me. Our life has certainly been a journey and a real-time textbook on overcoming fears and finding the way to faith. Thanks for figuring it out with me and for putting up with this process for the good part of three years.

To my three amazing daughters—Madiha, Zali and Zara—You are truly spectacular in every way. Your life is not normal; it's an extraordinary example of adventure and faith. The way you roll with the punches and approach life with passion ignites my faith. You have all sacrificed more in your young years than most will in a lifetime. God sees it all, and nothing goes unnoticed with Him. He is a rewarder of faith, and I want you to know that He is well pleased with you.

I must make special mention to Alexia Harris for your editing, formatting and grammatical expertise. Your commitment to this project—above and beyond normal assistant duties—is beyond appreciated. From punctuation to presentation, I thank you.

Thank you, Vance Roush, for the constant push and for coordinating content focus groups. The feedback from these groups was pivotal to the process and so appreciated. Thank you to all who contributed to the content focus groups. Your feedback was considered and helpful in communicating an often-complicated concept.

To my team of marketing, branding and design legends, thank you. Andrew Thomas, Katrina Macaraeg, Jo Pham, Britni Grellman and Francesca Chang— there really is not a more gifted team.

To the amazing cover designer, Jasmine Esmaili, thank you. Understanding the concept and interpreting the idea is not an easy task. I so appreciate all the creative meetings and many rounds of designs.

A huge thank-you to all the VIVE Church members who have made this journey a story. Each phase of the journey so far has been lived out in risk and reward. This is your story, and I can't wait to see what God does next.

Finally, thank you, Joshua, for your model of faith that we can glean from and grow from. Most of all, I want to thank my Lord and Savior, Jesus, the author and finisher of our faith. I'm praying that this book points people toward You as the hope and answer for a world so gripped with fear.

AUTHOR BIO

Adam Smallcombe and his wife, Keira, serve as the founders and lead pastors of VIVE Church, a global church that has grown from just seven people to thousands across five locations in the Bay Area, California, one location in Rome, Italy, and a vibrant online campus in just five years. Adam's bold faith to move his family from Australia to America to start VIVE Church is an example of the audacious faith he seeks to activate in others. Having studied at both C3 Bible College and Alphacrusis College, Adam is a sought-after speaker locally and globally, and has spoken at conferences, events, and leadership workshops. VIVE Church is part of the global C3 Movement, a movement focused on church planting and empowering leaders. Due to the influential nature of VIVE Church, Adam's preaching and the church as a whole have been featured on CNN, Buzzfeed, and BBC News outlets. His communication and pastoring style can be characterized by his humor and relentless determination to build people and pull out all God has for them.